CHILDREN IN NEED

INVESTMENT STRATEGIES FOR THE EDUCATIONALLY DISADVANTAGED

A STATEMENT BY THE RESEARCH AND
POLICY COMMITTEE OF THE COMMITTEE
FOR ECONOMIC DEVELOPMENT

Library of Congress Cataloging-in-Publication Data

Committee for Economic Development. Research and
    Policy Committee.
    Children in need.

    Includes bibliographies.
    1. Socially handicapped children—Education—United
States.   2. Federal aid to education—United States.
3. Industry and education—United States.   I. Title.
LC4091.C646   1987   371.96'7   87-21804
ISBN   0-87186-786-9 (lib. bdg.)
ISBN   0-87186-086-4 (pbk.)

First printing in bound-book form: 1987
Second printing (revised): 1989
Paperback: $10.50
Library binding: $12.50
Printed in the United States of America
Design: Stead Young & Rowe Inc.

COMMITTEE FOR ECONOMIC DEVELOPMENT
477 Madison Avenue, New York, NY 10022
(212) 688-2063
1700 K Street, N.W., Washington, D.C. 20006
(202) 296-5860

Photographs: Cover, clockwise from top left, Alex Harris,
    Rebecca Collette Chao, John P. Cavanagh, Roswell
    Angier, Roswell Angier, Alex Harris, Charles Harbutt,
    Charles Harbutt (center); all cover photos from Archive
    Pictures Inc. Chapter 1, Bobby Reynolds. Chapter 2,
    Robert Maust. Chapter 3, Mark Perrott. Chapter 4,
    Isaiah Wyner.

CONTENTS

CHILDREN IN NEED

INVESTMENT STRATEGIES FOR THE EDUCATIONALLY DISADVANTAGED

RESPONSIBILITY FOR CED STATEMENTS ON NATIONAL POLICY

The Committee for Economic Development is an independent research and educational organization of over two hundred business executives and educators. CED is nonprofit, nonpartisan, and nonpolitical. Its purpose is to propose policies that will help to bring about steady economic growth at high employment and reasonably stable prices, increase productivity and living standards, provide greater and more equal opportunity for every citizen, and improve the quality of life for all. A more complete description of CED appears on page 86.

All CED policy recommendations must have the approval of trustees on the Research and Policy Committee. This committee is directed under the bylaws to "initiate studies into the principles of business policy and of public policy which will foster the full contribution by industry and commerce to the attainment and maintenance" of the objectives stated above. The bylaws emphasize that "all research is to be thoroughly objective in character, and the approach in each instance is to be from the standpoint of the general welfare and not from that of any special political or economic group." The committee is aided by a Research Advisory Board of leading social scientists and by a small permanent professional staff.

The Research and Policy Committee does not attempt to pass judgment on any pending specific legislative proposals; its purpose is to urge careful consideration of the objectives set forth in this statement and of the best means of accomplishing those objectives.

Each statement is preceded by extensive discussions, meetings, and exchange of memoranda. The research is undertaken by a subcommittee, assisted by advisors chosen for their competence in the field under study. The members and advisors of the subcommittee that prepared this statement are listed on page viii.

The full Research and Policy Committee participates in the drafting of recommendations. Likewise, the trustees on the drafting subcommittee vote to approve or disapprove a policy statement, and they share with the Research and Policy Committee the privilege of submitting individual comments for publication, as noted on page 84 of this statement.

Except for the members of the Research and Policy Committee and the responsible subcommittee, the recommendations presented herein are not necessarily endorsed by other trustees or by the advisors, contributors, staff members, or others associated with CED.

RESEARCH AND POLICY COMMITTEE

PURPOSE OF THIS STATEMENT

Although much has been written on the need to improve our education system, recent reform efforts have largely bypassed the problems of the educationally disadvantaged — the 30 percent of children facing major risk of educational failure and lifelong dependency. In this statement we recommend strategies to meet the special needs of this growing educational underclass.

Children in Need: Investment Strategies for the Educationally Disadvantaged urges business leaders, educators, and policy makers to look beyond the traditional classroom boundaries and provide early and sustained intervention in the lives of these children. It calls for new partnerships among families, schools, businesses, and community organizations that can bolster the health, education, and well-being of the whole child, beginning with the formative years.

What is most compelling about this statement is the argument that improving the prospects for disadvantaged children is not an expense but an excellent investment, one that can be postponed only at much greater cost to society.

Our nation's need for a qualified work force to compete in the fast-changing global economy makes the recommendations in this report all the more urgent. This year nearly 1 million youngsters will leave high school without graduating, and most of them will be marginally literate and virtually unemployable.

LEADERSHIP FOR CHANGE

The report calls on the business community to take the lead in forming the coalitions of business, education, parent organizations, civic groups, and all levels of government that are required to meet this challenge. Business leaders are urged to speak out at the federal, state, and local levels for improved programs and necessary resources. The statement gives many concrete examples of effective corporate involvement in education that can be emulated by different types of businesses in all parts of the country.

Although all levels of government must strengthen their commitment to assisting children in need, federal leadership on this issue is crucial at this time to guide reform efforts and to inspire participation from the varied segments of our national community.

Improving the skills of disadvantaged children is a long and difficult process. It is an arduous political task to encourage cooperation among all levels of our government and a multiplicity of constituencies. Yet there is too much at stake to postpone this effort.

STRATEGY FOR REFORM

This report urges policy makers to adopt a three-part strategy for improving the prospects for disadvantaged children. These measures will have to be tailored to meet the needs of individual communities. We recommend:

■ **Prevention through Early Intervention** — programs that focus on children from birth to age five and on teenagers who are most at risk of premature parenthood;

■ **Restructuring the Foundations of Education** — changes that are needed in the structure, staffing, management, and financing of schools; and

■ **Retention and Reentry** — targeted programs that combine comprehensive educational, employment, health, and social services for students still in school and for dropouts.

CED's 1985 report *Investing in Our Children: Business and the Public Schools* called for higher educational standards, but recognized that disadvantaged children may need special help to achieve those standards. In the present report, CED identifies programs that will turn the tide of despair for those young people who lack the basic skills to participate in the social, political, and economic life of our society.

Literate, skilled, and adaptable people are our nation's most precious resource. *Children in Need* makes clear that as a society we must be willing to invest in building a better future for all of our children.

ACKNOWLEDGMENTS

On behalf of the Research and Policy Committee, I would like to express deep appreciation and thanks to Owen B. Butler, retired chairman of The Procter & Gamble Company, for his inspired and knowledgeable leadership of the Subcommittee on the Educationally Disadvantaged. Brad Butler's tireless efforts on behalf of education reform place him in the front ranks of national business leadership on this issue. We are also indebted to the subcommittee's vice chairman, Donna E. Shalala, president of Hunter College, for her expert guidance and energetic participation in the subcommittee's deliberations.

Special recognition is also due to the business leaders, education experts, and child care specialists, listed on page viii, who worked so diligently on this subcommittee; to project director Sol Hurwitz who brought extensive experience in public education to the organization and management of this project; and to project editor Sandra Kessler Hamburg who assembled the research and drafted the report with unusual skill and sensitivity.

In addition, I would like to acknowledge the important financial and intellectual contribution made by the foundations, listed on page 85, that have so generously supported this project.

William F. May
Chairman
Research and Policy Committee

CHAPTER ONE

INTRODUCTION AND SUMMARY OF RECOMMENDATIONS

For generations, the American Dream has been to live in freedom and to have the opportunity to pursue a satisfying life, reap the benefits of economic prosperity, and partake of the privileges and responsibilities of citizenship in the world's foremost democracy. But as we stand on the threshold of the twenty-first century, that dream is in jeopardy.

This nation cannot continue to compete and prosper in the global arena when more than one-fifth of our children live in poverty and a third grow up in ignorance. And if the nation cannot compete, it cannot lead. If we continue to squander the talents of millions of our children, America will become a nation of limited human potential. It would be tragic if we allow this to happen. America must become a land of opportunity — for every child.

Yet, the United States is creating a permanent underclass of young people for whom poverty and despair are life's daily companions. These are youths who cannot hold jobs because they lack fundamental literacy skills and work habits. They feel alienated from mainstream society, and they seldom participate in the democratic process. They cannot attain the living standard of most Americans because they are trapped in a web of dependency and failure.

The nation's public schools have traditionally provided a common pathway out of poverty and a roadway to the American Dream. But today, in too many communities, the schools are hard pressed to serve the needs of disadvantaged children. Beleaguered by powerful social forces swirling around them, the schools are ill equipped to respond to the multidimensional problems of poor and minority youngsters. The discrimination their students face and the alienation these children feel are often compounded by an archaic school structure and an unresponsive bureaucracy.

Children born into poverty often suffer from debilitating deprivations that seriously impair their ability to learn. Yet, most recent reforms have been targeted at the education system; rarely have they addressed the pressing needs of at-risk infants and toddlers and their families. We contend that reform strategies for the educationally disadvantaged that focus on the school system alone are doomed to continue to fail a substantial portion of these youths. Effective strategies must address the broader needs of these children from their earliest years.

Effective solutions to the problems of the educationally disadvantaged must include a fundamental restructuring of the school system. But they must also reach beyond the traditional boundaries of schooling to improve the environment of the child. An early and sustained intervention in the lives of disadvantaged children, both in school and out, is our only hope for breaking the cycle of disaffection and despair.

In recent years, the nation has made an unprecedented commitment to improving the quality of public education. Yet this first wave of reform has either ignored or underplayed the plight of the disadvantaged. Rather, its focus has been higher standards and tougher course requirements at the high school level.

Clearly, high standards and expectations are necessary if the high school diploma is once again to become a meaningful measure of educational achievement. Yet, as CED argued in its policy statement *Investing in Our Children: Business and the Public Schools* (1985), raising standards for all students without increased efforts to help children who may not meet those standards will go only partway toward realizing the nation's educational goals. It will leave a significant proportion of the population underskilled and probably unemployable.[1]

The second wave of reform has focused on improving the quality of the nation's teachers. *Investing in Our Children* called for "nothing less than a revolution in the role of the teacher and the management of the schools."[2] Upgrading the teaching profession is a prerequisite for improving the quality of the nation's schools, and it is critical for improving the education of disadvantaged children.

Now we call on the nation to embark upon a third wave of reform that gives the highest priority to early and sustained intervention in the lives of disadvantaged children.

In 1987, nearly 1 million young people will leave the nation's public schools without graduating. Most of them will be deficient in basic skills, marginally literate, and virtually unemployable. Another 700,000 will merely mark time in school and receive their diplomas but will be as deficient in meaningful skills and work habits as most dropouts.

Currently, fewer than 50 percent of high school seniors read at levels considered adequate for carrying out even moderately complex tasks, and 80 percent have inadequate writing skills. In a recent national study comparing mathematics skills in twenty nations, U.S. youngsters made a mediocre showing at best. Not only are our public schools failing to develop basic skills, they are also failing to develop the higher-order skills needed for the new information age.[3]

The nation can ill afford such an egregious waste of human resources. It makes no economic sense to educate half of our young people so poorly and to condemn the lowest-achieving students to the fringes of society. Allowing this to continue will not only impoverish these children, it will impoverish our nation — culturally, politically, and economically.

INVESTING IN THE FUTURE

Quality education is not an expense; it is an investment in the future of our nation. The economic miracle of Japan is no accident. The extraordinary value the Japanese place on education has succeeded in producing a population that is almost 100 percent literate and outscores all other nations on almost every test of academic achievement. It is inconceivable that the United States, with its vast resources, cannot educate its citizens as well as, or better than, Japan.

Failure to educate is the true expense — for both society and individuals. The most recent estimates suggest that each year's class of dropouts will cost the nation more than $240 billion in lost earnings and forgone taxes over their lifetimes.[4] This does not include the billions more for crime control and for welfare, health care, and other social services that this group will cost the nation. For each year that our schools fail to educate another million students, we lose billions of dollars that could have been put to better use. When costs are compared with benefits, early prevention and other education, health, and welfare programs designed to improve the lives of disadvantaged children yield impressive results (see Figure 1, pp. 6 and 7).

There are no quick or easy answers to the problems of the educationally disadvantaged. Although some of the reforms we advocate can be put in place now, others address fundamental, structural weaknesses in local and national policies toward children and youth and in our public schools. Effecting these longer-term reforms will take a sustained effort and a firm commitment over the years by a broad-based coalition of government, education, business, and community leaders. And it will require more money. **Any plan for major improvements in the development and education of disadvantaged children that does not recognize the need for additional resources over a sustained period is doomed to failure.***

In this policy statement, we emphasize the importance of a comprehensive and sustained approach to the needs of disadvantaged children within the context of their families, their schools, and their communities. State and local agencies whose actions affect disadvantaged children either directly or through their parents need to work closely with schools, community organizations, and businesses in order to minimize overlapping and piecemeal policies and practices. Welfare reform is a critical component of this comprehensive approach. Welfare policy should consider both the developmental and educational needs of children at risk, and it should help to reduce the dependency of future generations.

WHY BUSINESS CARES

The business community has made great strides in its involvement in education reform in the past several years. Equity, social justice, and the survival of our political and economic institutions compel us to address the needs of the disadvantaged on a broader scale.

If present trends continue without corrective actions, American business will confront a severe employment crisis. This scarcity of well educated and well qualified people in the work force will seriously damage this country's competitive position in an increasingly challenging global marketplace. Current projections point to a serious labor shortage in only a few years. By 1990, the impact of new technologies is expected to drive total private-sector demand for employment to 156.6 million jobs, nearly twice that in 1978. If these estimates are only close to the mark, there will be a shortage of over 23 million Americans willing and able to work.[5]

---

*See memorandum by DONALD M. STEWART, page 84.

Our industries will be unable to grow and compete because an expanding educational underclass will be unable to meet the demands of such jobs. Moreover, these young people will not enjoy the levels of literacy needed to make informed choices about their lives or to carry out the responsibilities and reap the rewards of citizenship in a democratic society.

Children of the poor have always been less likely to complete their education. However, in an earlier era of industrialization our nation could tolerate a sink-or-swim attitude toward those in school. Not only could American industry absorb massive numbers of unskilled laborers, but the nation's economy thrived on the endless supply of labor available. Until the 1950s, fewer than 50 percent of students graduated from high school. A strong back and a pair of deft hands could secure a decently paid factory job or help run a farm.

The technological revolution and intensified global competition have brought dramatic and irreversible changes to the job market. The nation's manufacturing sector has become more productive, but, at the same time, its jobs rely less and less on unskilled, manual labor. As production processes depend increasingly on computers and other sophisticated machinery, manufacturing jobs demand greater intellectual ability. Likewise, jobs in the growing service and knowledge industries, by their very nature, require more literate workers with good problem-solving skills — workers who have learned how to learn.

WHO ARE THE EDUCATIONALLY DISADVANTAGED?

Children are educationally disadvantaged if they cannot take advantage of available educational opportunities or if the educational resources available to them are inherently unequal (see "Children in Need: A Profile," page 8). Conservative estimates suggest that as much as 30 percent of the school population is educationally disadvantaged.[6]

These are truly children in need. Some are disadvantaged because they grow up in a deprived environment that slows their intellectual and social growth. Others may be raised with expectations that are very different from those that predominate in schools oriented toward middle-class values. Many schools, educators, and policy makers — whether consciously or unconsciously — expect children from poor, minority, or other disadvantaged backgrounds to fail, and such expectations can have a profoundly negative effect on both behavior and performance.

CHILDREN AND POVERTY

Some children born into poverty have the family support, the role models, and the determination to succeed in school despite their disadvan-

Preschool Education	Increased school success, employability and self-esteem; reduced dependence on public assistance.	$1 investment in quality preschool education returns $6.00 because of lower costs of special education, public assistance, and crime.	In 1985, there were 10.7 million children ages 3–5. 5.9 million of them were enrolled in public and non-public pre-primary programs. 453,000 children — fewer than 1 out of every 5 eligible — were participating in Head Start as of September 1987.
Compensatory Education	Achievement gains and maintenance of gains in reading and mathematics.	Investment of $750 for year of compensatory education can save $3,700 cost of repeating grade.	In 1985, 4.9 million children — an estimated 50% of those in need — received Chapter 1 services under the LEA Basic Grant Program.
Education for All Handicapped Children	Increased number of students receiving services and more available services.	Early educational intervention has saved school districts $1,560 per disabled pupil.	During 1985–1986, 4,121,104 children ages 3–21 were served under the State Grant program. The prevalence of handicaps in the population under age 21 is estimated to be 11.4% (9.5–10 million children).
Youth Employment and Training	Gains in employability, wages, and success while in school and afterwards.	Job Corps returned $7,400 per participant, compared to $5,000 in program costs (in 1977 dollars). FY 1982 service year costs for Youth Employment Training Program (YETP) were $4,700; participants had annualized earnings gains of $1,810.	During program year July 1986–June 1987, 64,954 youths were enrolled in Job Corps, and about 432,680 in Job Training Partnership Act (JTPA) Title IIA; 634,000 youths participated in summer youth programs. The annualized numbers of unemployed persons 16–21 years old in 1986 was 2,160,000.

Adapted from U.S. Congress. House of Representatives. Select Committee on Children, Youth, and Families. "Opportunities for Success: Cost Effective Programs for Children, Update 1988." 100th Congress, 2nd Session.

FIGURE I

Cost-Effective Programs for Children

	Benefits for Children	Cost Benefit	Participation
WIC—Special Supplemental Food Program for Women, Infants, and Children	Reduction in infant mortality and births of low birthweight infants.	$1 investment in prenatal component of WIC has saved as much as $3 in short-term hospital costs.	3.46 million participants — about 44% of those potentially eligible — received WIC services in March 1987, up by 300,000 since Spring 1985.
Prenatal Care	Reduction in prematurity, low birthweight births, and infant morbidity.	$1 investment can save $3.38 in cost of care for low birthweight infants.	24% of live births in 1985 were to mothers who did not begin prenatal care in the first trimester of pregnancy. The rate for white births was 21%, for black births 38%.
Medicaid	Decreased neonatal and infant morbidity and fewer abnormalities among children receiving Early Periodic Screening, Diagnosis, and Treatment (EPSDT) Services.	$1 spent on comprehensive prenatal care added to services for Medicaid recipients has saved $2 in infant's first year; lower health care costs for children receiving EPSDT services.	In FY 1983, an estimated 9.9 million dependent children under 21 were served by Medicaid, including 2.14 million screened under EPSDT. In calendar year 1983, there were 12.95 million children in families below the poverty line.
Childhood Immunization	Dramatic declines in incidence of rubella, mumps, measles, polio, diphtheria, tetanus, and pertussis.	$1 spent on Childhood Immunization program saves $10 in later medical costs.	In 1985, the total percent of children, ages 1–4, immunized against the major childhood diseases ranged from 73.8 for rubella to 87.0 for diphtheria-tetanus-pertussis. For those 5–14, percent immunized ranged from 85.3 for rubella to 93 for DTP. Smaller percentages of children in both age groups were immunized against polio, measles, and rubella in 1985 than in 1983.

tages; in fact, education has traditionally provided an escape from poverty for many children from poor families. Yet, poverty does correlate closely with school failure, especially where family structure has broken down as well. Poor students are three times more likely to become dropouts than students from more economically advantaged homes. Schools with higher concentrations of poor students have significantly higher dropout rates than schools with fewer poor students.[7] This is hardly surprising; children of the poor suffer more frequently from almost every form of childhood deficiency, including infant mortality, gross malnutrition, recurrent and untreated health problems, psychological and physical stress, child abuse, and learning disabilities.

As a group, children are now the poorest segment of the nation's popu-

---

CHILDREN IN NEED: A PROFILE

Although *poverty* and *minority* status are often used as synonyms for *disadvantaged*, a close examination of who fails in school reveals a situation that is not so easy to categorize. Children may fail in school for a wide variety of reasons.

- They may come to school poorly prepared for classroom learning or not yet ready developmentally for formal education.

- Their parents may be indifferent to their educational needs.

- They may be the children of teenagers who are ill equipped for parenting.

- They may have undiagnosed learning disabilities, emotional problems, or physical handicaps.

- They may have language problems or come from non-English-speaking homes.

- They may experience racial or ethnic prejudice.

- They may have access only to schools of substandard quality.

Forty percent of children in need are concentrated in urban inner cities, while the remaining 60 percent are dispersed throughout the rest of the education system. Many live in older suburbs and areas that are otherwise relatively affluent and in pockets of deep-seated rural poverty that exist in many parts of the country.[14]

---

lation. They are nearly seven times as likely to be poor as those over sixty-five.[8] Over 20 percent of all children under eighteen currently live in families whose incomes fall below the poverty line, and 25 percent of all children under six are now living in poverty. Although almost two-thirds of all poor children are white, both blacks and Hispanics are much more likely to be poor; 43 percent of black and 40 percent of Hispanic children live in poverty.[9] Black children are nearly three times as likely to live in poverty as white children, and the average black child can expect to spend five of the first fifteen years of childhood in an impoverished home.[10]

SINGLE-PARENT FAMILIES

Poverty is most highly pronounced for those children living in single-parent households headed by women. Children of single parents tend to do worse in school than those with two parents living at home, and their dropout rate is nearly twice as high.[11] In 1985, 66 percent of black children, over 70 percent of Hispanic children, and nearly half of all white children living in female-headed households lived in poverty. However, although one out of every six white children lives in a single-parent home, this condition has become the norm for black children, with 50 percent living in homes headed by single women.[12]

This trend seems to be continuing unabated. Last year, 74.5 percent of all black infants were born to unwed mothers, half of them to teenagers.[13]

CHILDREN OF CHILDREN

Children from poor and single-parent households are more likely than others to be children of teenage parents and to become teenage parents themselves. By age five, the children of teen parents already run a high risk of later unemployability. Not only do teen parents often lack employability skills; they also lack the necessary resources to begin developing their children's future parenting and employability skills.

THE DEMOGRAPHIC IMPERATIVE

Demographic trends dramatize the need to address seriously the plight of the disadvantaged; the sheer numbers and the growing proportion of the U.S. population that they represent are staggering. The percentage of both poor children and minorities in the United States has been rising steadily in recent years and will continue to climb in the foreseeable future. In 1984, 36 percent of the babies born in this country were members of minorities, and by the year 2000, the proportion of minority children under eighteen will be at least 38 percent.[15]

In 1985, minorities represented about 17 percent of the total U.S. population. By the year 2020, this proportion is expected to rise to more than one-third; if current demographic trends continue, a larger proportion of this group will be children from disadvantaged homes.[16]

AN EQUAL CHANCE

Many disadvantaged children persist against heavy odds to become successful learners and accomplished adults. More often than not, they prevail with the guidance and support of caring parents, teachers, counselors, and other adults who expect them to succeed and hold them to high standards. For many children from impoverished homes, racial and ethnic minorities, and immigrant families, our public schools can still serve as the surest route to rewarding lives.

But it is not surprising that disadvantaged children, many of whom enter school already damaged intellectually, emotionally, or physically, tend to perform worse than more affluent children on nearly every measure of educational attainment. We ask our schools to provide equal opportunity, and we expect them to do as good a job educating these children as they do children of affluence. Yet, if the educationally disadvantaged fail, the blame is often placed on the children themselves for their own supposed lack of intellectual ability or on their backgrounds.

Unfortunately, many communities with substantial numbers of poor and minority children have difficulty providing equitable access to educational resources. Wealthier school districts routinely spend more per pupil than schools that serve inner cities. But schools serving the disadvantaged need more resources, not less, because their students are in greater need. For children who come to school already handicapped by their circumstances, society needs to make a greater effort to provide adequate resources so that equal opportunity is not an empty concept.

INVESTMENT STRATEGIES FOR THE EDUCATIONALLY DISADVANTAGED

This is not the first time that the education of the disadvantaged has been targeted as a top national priority. Efforts have been made since the Great Society programs of the 1960s to improve the literacy levels and graduation rates of minorities and the poor. For over twenty years, federally funded Head Start and compensatory education programs under Title I of the Elementary and Secondary Education Act and later under Chapter I of the Education and Consolidation Act have demonstrated considerable success in narrowing the gap in reading and mathematics achievement between white and black elementary schoolchildren. But despite these early gains, the school dropout problem and the equally difficult problem of undereducation persist, particularly among society's most disadvantaged young people.

How should we respond? Clearly, we cannot continue to conduct business as usual. Incremental reform within the traditional confines of the nation's public schools simply cannot address the critical needs of this substantial segment of the school population.

Disadvantaged children are not all alike. Their problems vary with their family circumstances, the communities in which they live, and their age and level of development. **Programs and policies that are designed to help disadvantaged children improve their educational prospects must be tailored to meet the needs of the whole child within the context of school, family, and community.**

It is obvious that in many communities, especially those with high concentrations of disadvantaged families, the schools need to do more to overcome expectations that their students will fail. Schools that serve the disadvantaged will need to make special efforts to reach out to parents and the community to bridge the chasms that often separate them.

We urge policy makers to consider what we believe to be the three most important investment strategies for providing children in need with a better start and a boost toward successful learning: prevention through early intervention, restructuring the foundations of education, and retention and reentry.

PREVENTION THROUGH EARLY INTERVENTION

Learning is a cumulative process that begins at birth. The educational problems of disadvantaged children are especially obvious long before they begin formal education. It is less costly to society and to individuals to prevent early failure through efforts directed toward parents and children alike from prenatal care through age five. **Such efforts should include:**

- **Prenatal and postnatal care for pregnant teens and other high-risk mothers and follow-up health care and developmental screening for their infants.**

- **Parenting education for both mothers and fathers, family health care, and nutritional guidance.**

- **Quality child-care arrangements for poor working parents that stress social development and school readiness.**

- **Quality preschool programs for all disadvantaged three- and four-year-olds.**

We believe that to succeed in helping children at risk, we must respond to the needs of the whole child from prenatal care through adulthood. Such efforts must also involve the children's parents, who may themselves be disadvantaged and in need of support services to help them

learn how to prepare their children for a better future. We call for early and sustained intervention into the lives of at-risk children as the only way to ensure that they embark and stay on the road to successful learning.

RESTRUCTURING THE FOUNDATIONS OF EDUCATION

Good basic skills are the surest path to later academic and employment success. But as they are currently structured, most public schools have not been successful at ensuring that their disadvantaged students develop the academic skills and work habits they will need.

Children who are at risk of failing often attend schools that are at risk of failing their students. In such schools, which usually have high concentrations of poor and/or minority pupils, teachers and administrators may feel overwhelmed by the problems the children bring with them to the classroom, and they often expect these children to fail. Every student deserves to be guaranteed a chance to learn to the best of his or her ability. Accordingly, schools need to send this message to their students: "We care about you, and we expect you to succeed."

We believe that a great many of the nation's schools, particularly those that serve large numbers of disadvantaged students, need a radical redefinition of their purpose and structure. This will require a fundamental restructuring of the way most schools are organized, staffed, managed, and financed. As a society, we need to rethink the relationship of the school to the community.

Clearly, not all schools need such restructuring. Many are effectively educating their students to meet high standards, and many schools are already being redesigned along the lines discussed in greater detail in Chapter 3. However, too many schools that serve disadvantaged populations are opting for control rather than education, magnifying the alienation often experienced by the poor and minorities. Too many schools offer a large, impersonal environment that more closely resembles a factory than a haven for learning.

For schools that consistently fail their students, merely patching up the present system with more of the same may catch a few more students who have fallen through the cracks. But that is not enough. What these schools need is a new and restructured foundation for learning.

We believe that any plan to restructure public schools that serve the disadvantaged should include the following elements:

- **School-based management that involves principals, teachers, parents, students, and other school personnel in shared decision making and accountability for results. School management should encourage flexibility and innovation in the school curriculum, teaching methods, and organization.**

- Teachers who have made a commitment to working with the disadvantaged and who have expertise in dealing with children with multiple problems. Special support for those teachers needs to be made available by school districts and schools of education.

- Smaller schools and smaller classes that are designed not only to raise achievement levels but to increase quality contact with teachers and other adults.

- Support for preschool and child-care programs by the school system where appropriate for the community.

- Up-to-date educational technology integrated into the curriculum to provide new learning opportunities for students and additional pedagogical support for teachers.

- Support systems within the schools that include health services, nutritional guidance, and psychological, career, and family counseling.

- Increased emphasis on extracurricular activities that help build academic, social, or physical skills.

Restructuring strategies will also have to recognize the severe demographic shifts expected to occur within the teaching profession in the next decade. Experienced teachers will be retiring at the same time that a larger number of teachers will be needed. Despite some recent progress in recruiting more able college students and adults into schools of education and into the teacher work force, it is unlikely that there will be a large enough pool of well-qualified teacher applicants to fill all the expected vacancies. The scarcity of qualified minority teachers is particularly distressing.

In addition to the essential restructuring needed for schools serving the disadvantaged, we reaffirm the comprehensive strategy for basic reform of all schools set forth in *Investing in Our Children*. The cornerstone of that approach is a *bottom-up strategy* that focuses reform efforts at the point of learning: the individual school, the classroom, and the interaction between teacher and student (see "A Bottom-Up Strategy," page 14).[17] This strategy embodies the principles of school-based management and team decision making that are now being tried in Miami, New Haven, and Seattle, all of which have large numbers of disadvantaged students.

RETENTION AND REENTRY

Millions of students reach high school age already lost to the system, and a large proportion join the legions of dropouts who have few job prospects and little hope for the future. This group is the most difficult for which to make generalized prescriptions because their needs and skill levels vary greatly. **We recommend that programs targeted to students at risk of dropping out and those who have already left school should be carefully designed to meet the particular needs and deficiencies of these young people. Specifically, these programs should:**

- **Combine work experience with education in basic skills.***

- **Operate in an alternative setting that focuses on improving motivation, skills, and self-esteem.**

- **Provide continuity in funding and long-term evaluation of the success of the program and the progress of participants.**

WE KNOW ENOUGH TO ACT

Although we do not yet know how to prevent every disadvantaged child from failing, we do know what works for many. A broad variety of

---

A "BOTTOM-UP" STRATEGY

Our recommendations form a "bottom-up" strategy that views the individual school as the place for meaningful improvements in quality and productivity. This does not minimize the importance of states, localities, and the federal government in defining goals, setting priorities, and providing resources. Nor does it overlook the role that the state and local authorities must play when schools and school systems fail to meet minimum standards. The states should provide "top-down" guidance and support to local schools by establishing clear goals and high standards and by developing precise measuring tools to evaluate educational achievement. At the same time, the states should give the schools maximum freedom to develop and implement the methods that would best achieve those goals.

The focus of our recommendations, therefore, is on the individual school — its students, teachers, and administrators — and the community it serves. Our central concern is with the instructional process and the interaction between student and teacher. We give careful attention to the selection, training, motivation, compensation, and working conditions of the nation's present and future classroom teachers. We also place special emphasis on improving the management of the individual school, for we see many applicable lessons from business experience in handling professional employees and utilizing resources more effectively.

SOURCE: Committee for Economic Development, *Investing in Our Children: Business and the Public Schools,* page 7.

---

*See memorandum by DONALD M. STEWART, page 84.

high-quality programs targeted to the disadvantaged have demonstrated their success for children under widely divergent circumstances and at different points along the educational journey.* Here are some examples:

■ Quality Head Start and other preschool programs, such as the Perry Preschool Project in Ypsilanti, Michigan, have helped cut later dropout rates and welfare dependency in half.

■ The federally funded Chapter I remedial programs, which have been in existence for over twenty years, have successfully improved the reading and mathematics skills of millions of elementary school students.

■ Schools that stress participatory decision making involving principals, teachers, other school professionals, and parents have achieved impressive improvements in academic performance, behavior, and attendance.

■ For older youths, a number of successful programs provide comprehensive educational, psychological, career counseling, and health services that can help reduce alienation from school and society. Others offer a combination of academic learning, the opportunity to develop real job skills, and adult mentoring relationships.

Many of these programs are expensive, but for every $1 spent today to prevent educational failure, we can save $6 in the cost of remedial education, welfare, and crime further down the road.[18] The price of corrective action may be high, but the cost of inaction is far higher. According to Fred M. Hechinger, education columnist for *The New York Times,* "We have raised too many children without allowing them expectations of success, without giving them hopes of useful lives ahead. To continue to do so, in an era that has no economic or social use for the uneducated, is to court disaster."[19]

BUILDING PARTNERSHIPS: BUSINESS, EDUCATION, AND THE COMMUNITY

Business has an important stake in helping public schools improve the way they prepare young people for the future, and it has demonstrated its commitment to educational excellence through a broad spectrum of partnerships with the schools. It is now incumbent upon business to focus its collaborative activities more sharply on disadvantaged children, so that quality education is available to every child, and every child is prepared to succeed in school.

---

*See memorandum by ROBERT A. CHARPIE, page 84.

In developing corporate strategies for the educationally disadvantaged, neither the guidelines for corporate involvement nor the major types of partnerships need to differ significantly from those that already exist. However, the deeply ingrained problems of the disadvantaged will require collaborations that reach beyond the traditional boundaries of public education. This problem offers a new challenge to business to help bring together many different groups within the community, including schools, parents, community agencies, and local government, that can identify and strengthen effective existing projects and initiate promising new programs. Business can also play a critical role in helping to guide community resources into programs that represent the best available investments and yield the most far-reaching results.

However, it is important that our concern with the economic benefits of educating the disadvantaged does not obscure the human dimensions of the problem. Business leaders, governors, state legislators, school officials, and teachers need to show disaffected young people that they care about them as individuals and want them to succeed. Evidence suggests that small programs work best. Massive programs wrapped in bureaucratic anonymity and red tape run the risk of depersonalizing a problem that involves basic human needs.

For effective partnerships, each side must fully understand what the other has to offer and develop a realistic view of what can be accomplished. The goal of partnerships should be to engage children, teachers, administrators, parents, and business executives in efforts designed to improve the children's performance, broaden their horizons, and demonstrate an ongoing commitment from the community.

Business can play a pacesetting role in providing opportunities for parents to participate in their children's schooling, involving employees in volunteer activities on behalf of the schools, helping teachers and administrators develop and hone new skills, developing mentoring relationships with individual students, and offering career counseling, tutorial services, and opportunities for entry into the job market.

We urge business to become a driving force in the community on behalf of public education and a prime advocate of educational initiatives for disadvantaged youngsters. Such advocacy should include supporting local education funds, encouraging employee participation on local school boards, and speaking out forcefully on behalf of public education at the local, state, and national levels.

The business community should take the lead in encouraging and supporting higher funding levels where they are needed both for early prevention programs and for the public education system. Business can also help to identify proven programs and work on the national, state, and local levels to ensure that these programs receive adequate financial support. Examples of such programs are Head Start and Chapter I, which still enroll only a small percentage of the eligible children who need them.

Another important issue that can benefit from increased business advocacy is the need for basic capital improvements in many older urban school districts and rural areas. Many schools, particularly in areas with high concentrations of disadvantaged children, are experiencing severe overcrowding and physical decay due to long-deferred maintenance. If schools are to become inviting and effective places where children can learn, such costly but necessary physical improvements will have to be seriously considered by policy makers and the public.

WHO IS RESPONSIBLE?

Solutions will require the combined efforts of many institutions: the public schools, businesses, foundations, community agencies, and every level of government. Development and implementation of many of the investment strategies we recommend will require both significant increases in funding and better targeting in order to assure that the necessary resources reach those children most in need. But although the problem of educating the disadvantaged is national in scope, progress is best achieved at the state and local levels, and most effectively within the individual school.

FEDERAL RESPONSIBILITIES

We believe that the federal government needs to reaffirm its long-standing commitment to ensuring the disadvantaged access to quality education. Without equity, there can be no real excellence in education.

The federal government can set the tone and direction for change by establishing and funding demonstration projects in early childhood education, dropout prevention, and other programs targeted to improving the quality of education for children in need. Although we do not envision that all such programs will be permanently funded at the federal level, federal leadership is needed at this time to help point the way for states that do not currently support preschool education or other targeted programs.

Because Chapter I remedial reading and mathematics programs and Head Start programs have had demonstrable success, we urge that federal funding for these programs be brought up to levels sufficient to reach all eligible children. Moreover, continuous assessment and tracking of data are needed to assure that reforms and special programs, such as Chapter I and Head Start, operate effectively. This is best accomplished at the

national level; therefore, it is more important than ever for the federal government to fund high-quality research, development, evaluation, and technical assistance for Chapter I, Head Start, and related programs. Educational researchers need to develop a new generation of compensatory education models, and school districts sorely need hands-on technical assistance from those who know how to implement and evaluate currently effective models and those that are emerging.

STATE AND LOCAL GOVERNMENTS

Despite the almost three-decade commitment of the federal government to improving the education of the disadvantaged, state governments have always had the primary responsibility for public education. The states have clearly taken the lead in the current wave of education reform, and they have reasserted their historic role on behalf of public schools.

The states have given economic development a very high priority, and states with the richest pool of human resources will be most able to attract and retain business activity. Education is a key component of economic development, and the states have begun paying for an increasing portion of the education bill. In exchange, they have come to expect higher performance from local school districts and have increased both educational requirements and regulations governing how these new standards should be met.

Although state involvement in education reform has had on the whole a very positive effect on the quality of education, we repeat the recommendation (which we first proposed in *Investing in Our Children*) that states resist the temptation to supplant local authority to a substantial degree. State-directed programs tend to create layers of bureaucracy, produce onerous and ill-defined regulations, and obscure the plight of individual students whose welfare is the ultimate objective of these programs. Local school districts and individual schools should be provided with enough discretionary power so that programs are kept small in scale, remain manageable and flexible, and are able to be individualized.

Local school districts need to be held accountable to the community and to the education authority of their state. In individual schools, accountability for student performance should extend to principals, teachers, and parents.

The states have become the educational watchdogs of our time. States have taken the lead and assumed the responsibility for maintaining educational standards. They should also assure that adequate and appropriate funding reaches those school districts whose students are most in need of additional support.

*   *   *

Children who are deprived of a decent education are disadvantaged in a society that requires high levels of literacy and skills to succeed. Children who are not adequately served by the public school system are truly in need. We know that the costs of providing a quality education to all of the nation's disadvantaged children will be high; but if we fail to act, the true costs will be many times higher. We must view quality education as an investment, not an expense.

Ironically, we now know how to save about half of the young people who fall prey to illiteracy, unemployment, and teenage pregnancy. Twenty years of research on preschool education has demonstrated the effectiveness of early prevention.

Such programs will be expensive. But if the nation defers the expense of preventive programs during the formative years, it will incur much higher and more intractable costs for older children who have already experienced failure. Even so, we cannot limit our efforts to only one group of disadvantaged children; both economic and humanitarian considerations impel us to find ways to expand our preventive efforts, improve basic education for all students, and enhance the chances of those in and out of school who have already been failed by the system.

CHAPTER TWO

PREVENTING FAILURE: POLICIES FOR INFANCY THROUGH PRESCHOOL

The seeds of educational failure are planted early. Children who are born into poverty or overly stressful family circumstances often suffer from a wide variety of physical and emotional problems that can delay normal social and intellectual development or impair their ability to function effectively in the typical public school setting.

Although the ultimate causes of educational failure may vary significantly from child to child, most educators believe that potential dropouts can be clearly identified by third grade. The patterns of behavior that lead to school failure and dropping out begin to appear during infancy and the toddler years. Without early intervention, such children will have difficulty taking advantage of the learning opportunities available in elementary and secondary school. It is therefore likely that many otherwise bright children will have their talents lost to themselves and society.

Unfortunately, *dropout prevention* is a concept usually reserved for programs targeted to students at the point of dropping out — high school. Furthermore, dropout-prevention strategies rarely consider the high percentage of students who float through school earning a diploma but failing to develop more than the most rudimentary skills. Teenagers rarely make a sudden, conscious decision to leave school at the age of fifteen or sixteen; the act of dropping out is the culmination of years of frustration and failure. Teenagers do not necessarily "drop out"; rather, they "drift away" as school holds less purpose and promise for their lives.

EARLY INTERVENTION

Happily, there is now a growing public awareness of the need to work with at-risk children before they enter the formal classroom setting, and quality preschool education is emerging as a leading issue. About half the states are now investing considerable resources to deliver preschool education to those children who can benefit most from such a head start.

Many states have rushed to create programs where none previously existed or are moving to improve the quality of and increase access to Head Start and other preschool programs and to existing kindergarten programs. In certain states and communities, business has played a key role in the establishment or expansion of these programs.

In 1986, the nation spent $264 billion on education for children age six and older, while it spent only about $1 billion for educating children five years old and younger.[1] States with the largest numbers of preschoolers in poverty are the ones most likely to have state-funded preschool programs. The eight states with the largest numbers of poor preschoolers — together they accounted for 48 percent of the nation's impoverished preschoolers in 1986 — all have state-funded early childhood programs.[2]

Unfortunately, these activities, however promising, are reaching only a small percentage of the children who need extra help to reach the higher standards now being set by almost every state education authority. Preschool programs for the disadvantaged, such as Head Start, reach fewer than 20 percent of eligible children. [3]

Yet, high-quality preschool programs have a demonstrated record of success in breaking the cycle of failure for children from severely disadvantaged families. Such programs as the Perry Preschool Project in Ypsilanti, Michigan, and the Harlem Head Start Program in New York City have helped to reduce by about half later dropout behavior, criminal involvement, welfare dependency, and the need for remedial education. Nevertheless, even if every state were to provide quality preschool to every disadvantaged four-year-old, this additional year of education would not be a cure-all for later educational failure and dropout behavior. Despite the obvious advantages of quality preschool, one additional year of education cannot make up for several years of poverty, deprivation, parental neglect, and racial prejudice.

In any consideration of the educational needs of disadvantaged children, our nation must look for solutions that reach beyond the traditional boundaries of public schooling to include programs for at-risk infants and toddlers. **We believe that for children in need, we must begin to view the needs of the whole child from prenatal care through adulthood. Such efforts must also involve parents who may themselves be disadvantaged and in need of support services to help them learn how to prepare their children for a better future. We call for early and sustained intervention into the lives of at-risk children as the best way to ensure that they embark and stay on the road to success.** We are particularly concerned that those children who begin their lives handicapped by poverty and family background receive the extra societal support that their circumstances demand.

Experts in child development and medicine agree that although family intervention can be useful at any point during the preschool years, the earlier the intervention, the less costly and less risky it is. From the standpoint of cost-effectiveness, for example, one expert notes that prenatal care for a pregnant teen can cost as little as $600 per client, whereas intensive care for low-birth-weight babies or premature infants can easily cost $1,000 a day. [4]

THE DISADVANTAGED INFANT: PREVENTING DEVELOPMENTAL PROBLEMS

A key reason that disadvantaged children have such a high rate of educational failure is that they often lag in physical and psychological development and may be unprepared to meet the demands of academic learning.

Estimates of the proportion of children lacking readiness for formal schooling vary. Some studies suggest that as many as one-third of the children eligible to enter kindergarten are not ready to do so. Another study concluded that as many as 50 percent of youngsters are placed in grades one or two years ahead of their developmental age.[5]

Although school readiness is a major objective of most preschool programs, for children in need this developmental lag begins even before birth and is exacerbated during the infant and toddler years. Some of the reasons include:

- **Low birth weight** — Medical evidence demonstrates that low birth weight is often linked to youth of the mother, inadequate medical care, and inattention to proper nutrition. Low birth weight is tied to a variety of learning disorders, including hyperactivity and dyslexia.

- **Emotional deprivation** — Many youngsters who have children are not prepared for the emotional burden of caring for them. Many babies receive sporadic maternal attention, which makes it difficult for them to feel secure in their world.

- **Chaotic home lives** — These children often must compete for attention with other siblings, young aunts and uncles, and other family members. In many inner cities, families double and triple up in small apartments, often illegally, creating even more crowding and chaos. Teenage mothers and their babies now make up a significant proportion of homeless families living in shelters, and many of these babies have never known a stable home.

- **Drug dependency** — Many disadvantaged mothers are drug users who inadvertently impair the health of their unborn children. In addition, the atmosphere of a home where parents are regular drug users exacerbates many of the other problems that afflict disadvantaged youngsters.

THE PARENT-CHILD RELATIONSHIP

The National Center for Clinical Infant Programs notes that despite changes in family demographics, today's infants and toddlers have exactly the same needs that babies have always had:[6]

- Adequate nutrition

- Safe shelter

- Appropriate health care and supervision

- Nurturing by familiar adults who are responsive to the uniqueness of the individual child from the moment of birth

Pediatric experts know that the attachment of infant to mother is a biological mechanism for survival. These bonds help individuals develop a sense of personal worth, the ability to interact with others in a mutually supportive environment, and the ability to form attachments apart from the mother. Mothers who are overstressed may have difficulty caring for or accepting their infants, and their children may have serious difficulty satisfying their deep psychological need for attachment. This situation is compounded when several children in the home are competing for inadequate parental or caretaker attention.

Under most circumstances, parents are the best care-givers for their children. Parents want the best for their children, even when they themselves lack adequate parenting skills, as is the case with most unmarried teenage mothers and fathers. By providing appropriate education in care-giving for parents, society is certain to circumvent some of the problems that children from deprived homes generally bring with them to school.

Medical evidence suggests that children are remarkably resilient: with the appropriate remedial help they will bounce back from early traumas and deprivation. This view certainly supports the value of later intervention and the need for a broad spectrum of compensatory programs in the elementary grades, such as the federally supported Chapter I programs that have been in place in designated schools for over twenty years.

However, we would argue for the earliest possible intervention with at-risk families for reasons of both compassion and cost-effectiveness. Just as it is less expensive to provide prenatal care to pregnant teenagers than it is to care for a premature or low-birth-weight baby, it is also apparent that the longer ameliorative efforts are postponed, the more difficult, extensive, and costly they become.

CHILDREN OF CHILDREN

Of all the demographic issues currently facing the nation, none is as serious as the alarming increase in unmarried teenage parenthood and the attendant poverty and dependency such families usually experience. Teenage motherhood stunts two lives at once. Girls who have babies at age fifteen, sixteen, or even younger frequently become permanent dropouts from school and society, forever dependent on government support. Children born to teenage mothers face special health risks. They are often born prematurely or suffer from low birth weight, conditions that predispose them to developmental retardation and a variety of learning disabilities.

Of every six babies born in the United States today, one will be the child of a teenage mother. In the past, these young mothers might have given up their newborns for adoption; but 96 percent now keep their babies. These girls are very often the second or third generation of teenage mothers in their families.[7]

Although the teenage pregnancy problem is most acute for black teens, this is not just a minority problem. In 1986, almost 30 percent of black girls under the age of nineteen became pregnant, and half of them gave birth. Yet, since 1970, the number of babies born to unwed white teenagers has more than doubled, surpassing the number born to black teenage mothers.[8]

Other statistics on teen parenthood highlight the tremendous costs of this phenomenon to both individuals and society.[9]

- Over 50 percent of the welfare expenditures in this country goes to families in which the mother began her parenting as a teenager.

- From 18 to 25 percent of all teenage mothers will become pregnant with their second child within one year of having their first. Up to 70 percent will have a second child within two years of the first.

- The United States has the highest rate of teenage pregnancy among all developed countries — seven times that of the Netherlands, three times that of Sweden, and more than twice that of Great Britain and Canada. The actual birth rate for American teenagers is four times that of Canada.

- Fewer than 50 percent of teenage mothers graduate from high school, and teen fathers are 40 percent less likely to graduate than their peers who are not parents.

- Nearly one-third of sexually active teenagers use no contraception; thus, more than 1.5 million young women are exposed to a high risk of unintended pregnancy.

The growing rate of teenage pregnancy has many causes, including:

- Lack of self-esteem and hope for the future

- Peer pressure

- Boredom and too much free time

- Ignorance about reproduction and the consequences of sexual activity

- Ignoring or misunderstanding the use of contraception and a lack of information about where to obtain contraceptive services

- Psychological need for love and a sense of purpose

- Lack of communication with parents and other adults

- A desire to assume adult roles

- Lack of knowledge about the responsibility of being a parent

Effectively addressing this problem is difficult for a variety of reasons, not the least of which is the ongoing national debate on the morality of providing family planning and contraceptive information and services to minors in the school setting. Sex education and information about related health services, when framed within the context of community values, can be a valuable tool in a broad-based strategy to reduce teen pregnancy and childbearing. In implementing sex education programs, however, schools need to work with parents and community leaders to develop programs that are compatible with the values of the community.

Another severe handicap to solving this problem is the way in which most services are delivered. For those most in need or least able to cope, services are generally designed as a device for crisis intervention. Prevention is not usually a part of this design. According to a report on teen pregnancy by the state of New York: "This delayed approach to services has hindered efforts to develop a systematic network of supports and services which promote positive youth and family development."[10]

Clearly, teen motherhood is both a cause and a consequence of dropping out. Girls who become pregnant are often bored or turned-off by education to begin with. For many who intended to graduate, get a job, and even go on to college, their choices become limited by the practical necessity of caring for their children and the general lack of support mechanisms beyond welfare.

The growing phenomenon of children having children presents society and the public schools with multiple, inextricably intertwined issues. First, there is the problem of teen motherhood itself. How can teen pregnancy be prevented? And for those teens who do become parents, what support services are needed to discourage further childbearing and prevent them from becoming permanent wards of the state? Second, how do we start their babies on the road to healthy physical, emotional, and intellectual development so that they do not become part of a multigenerational poverty culture?

A FIVE-STEP PROGRAM

The problem of teen parenthood needs to be addressed through a combination of policies and programs at the federal, state, and local levels. This is not an issue that lends itself to easy answers or simple solutions. It will require a combination of resources from both public and private sectors and a willingness to extend the boundaries of traditional education. Public schools and community agencies will need to work together to provide a combination of academic education, parenting education, health care, child care, and employment services.

We recommend a five-step program that can create a success-oriented environment for both young mothers and their children and prevent the problem from becoming multigenerational.

1. Keep pregnant teens and those with babies in school. Developing the skills that will help them get and keep decently paid jobs is the best deterrent to repeat pregnancies and a lifetime of dependency.

2. Emphasize parenting education. Programs should instruct teen mothers — and also young fathers who ought to share the responsibility of parenthood — in the physical and emotional care of their children.

3. Provide both prenatal and postnatal health care and nutritional guidance for mothers and babies. Low birth weight, a common problem in babies of girls who become pregnant before the age of seventeen, leads to health problems and learning disabilities. Young girls from disadvantaged homes are more likely to be malnourished in general, and for mothers dependent on public assistance, there is often not enough knowledge or resources available to provide adequate nutrition for their children. The only place where many disadvantaged children see a doctor is in the local hospital emergency room after a minor health problem has become serious. Preventive care is essential for keeping children healthy.

4. Provide day care for young mothers in school, preferably onsite. The policy toward young mothers used to be that help ended at delivery. We now know that that approach only exacerbates the problem. It will be easier to keep young mothers in school if they can be near their children. This is also the best logistical solution because onsite facilities provide the ideal opportunity to use day care for ongoing parenting education and for providing a stimulating environment for infants and toddlers.

5. Replicate successful programs in the middle grades (six, seven, and eight) that can motivate young people to make plans for careers other than early parenting.

Research indicates that when multiple-risk mothers begin their child rearing as teenagers, both they and their children do worse with each subsequent pregnancy. However, when intervention takes place with young mothers when they have their first child, such intervention creates a better family structure not only for the first child but for any subsequent children.

Even families with more than three generations of marginal coping and a history of distrust of traditional services can benefit from ongoing preventive intervention that helps them to develop the skills needed to function competently.[11]

The Beethoven Project in Chicago, sponsored by Chicago businessman Irving B. Harris and funded by a combination of public and private resources, is an example of such a parent-child approach. It operates in a high-poverty public housing project that is home to a large number of teen mothers. The Beethoven Project (described in more detail in Chapter 4) works with teen mothers and their children from early in the pregnancy until the child enters kindergarten. Two other programs that work with pregnant teens and adolescent parents to provide them and their children with a better start in life are those of the Children's Aid Society in New York City (see page 29) and the New Futures School in Albuquerque, New Mexico (see page 30).

Family planning professionals working in less developed countries have determined that the most effective form of birth control is education that increases aspirations and provides concrete job skills. Indeed, young mothers in this country who have participated in early intervention programs are more likely to have fewer children and to be less dependent on welfare.

SUPPORT SYSTEMS FOR POOR FAMILIES AND WORKING PARENTS

Not all disadvantaged children are the children of teen parents. Children in need come from a broad spectrum of family circumstances, and their problems require a flexible policy response on the part of schools and communities. While many parents of disadvantaged children have few practical job skills and may not have the ability or inclination to work, many others work hard at low-level jobs in order to provide their families with the basic necessities of life.

Whether they have two parents who work, or whether they live in single-parent homes, these children live in families that must struggle to meet their basic needs. Their families can provide few of the advantages generally taken for granted in middle-class homes. In many such families, little or no English may be spoken, and the parents are often fighting great odds to keep off the welfare rolls and provide a better life for their children. These children can face formidable obstacles to their success in school.

Because many such families may be technically above the poverty

THE CHILDREN'S AID SOCIETY/HUNTER COLLEGE PREGNANCY PREVENTION PROGRAM

Started in 1985, the Children's Aid Society's Teen Pregnancy Program is a pilot project located in central Harlem, directed by Hunter College professor Michael Carrera. The program emphasizes personal development as the surest prevention for teenage pregnancy. This past year, there were sixty-six teenagers between thirteen and seventeen years old, both male and female, and thirty young parents enrolled in the program.

Motivated by the belief that low self-esteem and self-confidence are the primary causes of pregnancy and childbearing among inner-city teens, the program seeks to bolster self-image by helping minority teenagers formulate value systems and career goals.

The program, which is taught over a series of fifteen two-hour sessions after school and during the evenings, has seven components:

■ **Family Life and Sex Education** — This involves role playing, films, readings, tests, and communication experiences.

■ **Career and Job Readiness** — Part-time and full-time summer jobs are provided at the society as well as at some private firms. Teens also agree to deposit a portion of each paycheck at a local bank.

■ **Self-Esteem Enrichment through the Performing Arts** — Weekly workshops with the National Black Theatre explore issues related to teen pregnancy.

■ **Health and Medical Services** — Physical examinations are provided at a local hospital, and a full-time nurse and two adolescent health specialists conduct health and medical services one day each week.

■ **Sports and Recreation** — Designed to foster discipline and self-control, sports are taught as an important part of a healthy life-style.

■ **Homework Help Program** — All of the participants are given an academic assessment of educational strengths and weaknesses, and public school teachers work with them three times each week to strengthen problem areas.

■ **Guaranteed Access to College** — Students who complete high school (and in some cases their parents as well) are guaranteed admission to Hunter College.

To date, not one of the sixty-six participants in the program has become a parent, dropped out of school, or developed a drug or alcohol problem.

Contact: Michael Carrera, The Children's Aid Society, 130 E. 101 Street, New York, NY 10029

NEW FUTURES SCHOOL

The New Futures School offers comprehensive educational, health, counseling, vocational, and child-care services for pregnant teens and adolescent parents. An alternative school within the Albuquerque, New Mexico, public school system, New Futures School is supported by a nonprofit, community-based organization, New Futures, Inc.

The goal of the school is to help school-age parents make responsible, informed decisions, complete their education, have healthy babies, and become well adjusted and self-sufficient. Since its creation in 1970, New Futures School has provided services for nearly 4,000 adolescent parents.

The program's in-school services are divided into two departments: the Perinatal Program, which serves the teen who enters the school during her pregnancy and remains until the end of the semester in which her child is born, and the Young Parent's Center, which is designed to serve school-age mothers who cannot successfully participate in a regular school program following the birth of their child.

The school offers a full range of support services. Health services include individual health counseling, group health instruction, and nutrition counseling. Each young mother's health is monitored throughout her pregnancy and in the two weeks following delivery.

Counseling and social services are integral components of the program. Each student is involved in group counseling once a week, and counselors are also available on an individual basis for students with special needs.

The school operates three onsite child-care facilities. In addition to child care, these facilities provide the staff with an opportunity to observe the parenting skills of the young mothers, give mothers time to breast-feed, and provide experience for students in classes on child care and development.

Vocational services are also available in the form of skill training for finding and keeping a job. Students who successfully complete the program are provided with a listing of potential employers.

New Futures also operates an outreach program that targets alienated youths in low-income areas. The school responds to requests from schools, churches, and community agencies for presentations aimed at reducing teen pregnancy, and it sponsors "Family Talks," a training series for parents of preteens that is designed to teach the parents how to provide their children with sex education.

Contact: Caroline Gaston, Principal/Program Coordinator, New Futures School, Albuquerque Public Schools, 2120 Louisiana Boulevard N.E., Albuquerque, NM 87110 guidelines set by federal or local authorities, they often are not eligible for additional benefits, such as health care or food stamps, that would help them keep their children physically healthy or provide adequate nutrition. For parents in marginal, low-paying jobs, the loss of nonmonetary benefits may act as a financial disincentive to working. Yet, we know that school dropouts disproportionately come from families on the welfare rolls.

We recommend that support systems be mobilized on behalf of disadvantaged families and children. Several types of support services have been identified as particularly useful for poor parents.

■ **Home Visitor Programs.** This support service can have a meaningful influence on parent behavior. These programs can increase a family's use of preventive services, decrease child abuse, and reduce hospitalization for neonatal intensive care. They can also help to improve the development of children and the health habits and nurturing skills of family members. Chicago's Beethoven Project employs home visitors who themselves live in the housing project and were on welfare. By providing support to younger women and their children, many of the older women who act as home visitors are becoming motivated to stay off the welfare rolls themselves.

■ **Parent-Child Centers.** At parent-child centers, young mothers are taught to become effective teachers of their own children and to develop good mother-child relationships.

■ **Family Resources Programs.** These programs strive to meet certain basic needs in ways that fit particular family circumstances. In addition to providing parenting education, they connect parents with community resources that can create opportunities for employment or training as well as provide health care, food, shelter, and clothing.

QUALITY CHILD CARE FOR POOR WORKING PARENTS

In 1985, more than one-quarter of all impoverished mothers with children under the age of six were in the labor force; whether they were single parents or part of a two-parent household made little difference in their rate of work force participation.[12]

High rates of labor force participation by women with children have existed for many years. Yet, the need for better methods of child care is an issue that is only now reaching the spotlight. Current data indicate that quality care for infants and toddlers is insufficient for most American parents, regardless of where they stand on the socioeconomic scale. Statistics on the availability and use of day-care services are sketchy at best. In 1982, private home care accounted for 77 percent of infant care. Fewer than 10 percent of infants of working mothers were placed in day-care centers. As of June 1985, 45 percent of infants and toddlers under age three were cared for by a relative — 27 percent in their own home and 18 percent in a relative's; 24 percent were cared for in family day-care facilities. [13]

Even middle-class parents have limited choices when it comes to providing adequate full-day care for their children, and many are financially hard pressed to find affordable quality care. In both poor and not-so-poor homes, very young children are often left in the care of another child who may not be much older, because their parents cannot afford the extra cost of day care. For many poor parents, particularly poor single mothers, the lack of safe, affordable day-care options combined with existing welfare policies creates a climate in which it is better not to work. Unfortunately, this situation serves to keep those on public assistance firmly entrenched within the welfare system.

For the children of these parents, the quality of their early care places them in additional jeopardy. With child-care services that are affordable, safe, and of high quality, more poor parents could be encouraged to seek work outside the home and become self-supporting or at least able to contribute partially to the support of their families. Such a change in their situation could have a two-fold positive impact. Working at productive employment provides people with enhanced self-esteem and increased economic power. This, in turn, tends to increase their aspirations for their children. In addition, their children begin to make the connection between education and work and find improved role models in the home.

Child care needs to be of good quality if it is to have value. It should not be strictly custodial; rather, it should provide intellectual stimulation and opportunities to learn and reinforce language and socialization skills. Good programs should provide high staff-to-child ratios, an appropriate developmental curriculum, and the expertise to address developmental problems. In order to encourage parents at the low end of the socioeconomic ladder to work, child-care facilities should provide a physically safe environment and flexible hours to accommodate parents who work either part time or full time. Day-care programs can be located either in the neighborhoods where families reside or near worksites. In either case, they should be accessible by public transportation.

Funding for child care for preschool-age children of the poor is of necessity a public responsibility, whether at the federal, state, or local level. Business can assist, however, by contributing its expertise in the field of referral services, which many corporations are now providing to their own employees. Beyond that, businesses in collaboration with civic organizations can reach out to poor parents in the community to increase their access to information on the availability and quality of day care.

PRESCHOOL: A SOUND INVESTMENT

Preschool programs that target the disadvantaged and stress developmental learning and social growth represent a superior educational investment for society. Preschool programs have become an educational priority in almost half the states. Texas, New York, California, and Washington are making universal preschool for the disadvantaged a key element of their statewide education reform efforts.

The impressive results of one of the most highly praised and duplicated preschool programs, the Perry Preschool Program (Ypsilanti, Michigan), indicates that the continued trend toward establishment of similar quality programs would be one of the most worthwhile educational investments the nation could make. Nonetheless, a close examination of the data from both the Perry Preschool Program and the Harlem Head Start study in New York City discloses several caveats concerning the efficacy of such programs. Although most children benefited, the programs did not provide enough to save all of those who participated from future distress. About one-third of the children who participated still required expensive remedial education, developed delinquent behavior leading to eventual incarceration, and became unemployable high school dropouts. Preschool programs have to be carefully designed so that they provide a meaningful and truly enriching experience for their participants.

Despite these qualifications, we strongly support quality preschool education for disadvantaged three- and four-year-olds and recommend that the nation continue to expand these programs until every eligible child has the opportunity to be enrolled.

PRESCHOOL QUALITY

In the rush to establish these programs on a broad scale, it is imperative that state legislators and educational policy makers maintain a clear vision of what constitutes a *quality* preschool program.

A comparative study of the long-term effects of fourteen different preschool programs conducted by the Consortium for Longitudinal Studies at Cornell University concluded that most high-quality programs were effective in raising achievement and IQ scores and improved self-esteem for the children who participated. The project concluded that any well-designed, professionally supervised program to stimulate and socialize infants and young children from poor minority families is effective. The project also identified the common characteristics of the most successful programs:[14]

- Meticulous planning and clearly stated objectives

- A high ratio of instructional staff to students

- Instructional objectives that are closely tied to program objectives

- High intensity of treatment

- Rigorous training of instructional personnel in the methods and content of the program

Among its other purposes in providing an intellectual head start for disadvantaged children, preschool should also place a priority on promoting healthy social development. Preschool provides an excellent opportunity for building the foundations for the kinds of character traits that can lead to success in formal schooling and in the workplace. Through play and socialization, preschoolers can learn to get along with others, build self-confidence and a better self-image, and gain greater control over their environment.

The preschool program run by the Ysleta School District in El Paso, Texas, provides an excellent example of how such a program can be developed to meet the special needs of the disadvantaged community it serves. Parental involvement is a specific focus of this program, and the district enlisted the help of community leaders to get the parents, many of whom were as young as twenty or twenty-one, to come to the school with their children. The district used the opportunity to teach parenting skills to these young parents. The school also established an outreach program that sent school personnel door-to-door in the community to enlist the support of parents and elicit their input into the school system. There are now about 2,000 preschoolers voluntarily enrolled in the program by their parents, about two-thirds of all those eligible (see "Ysleta Pre-Kinder Center Program," page 35).

PRESCHOOL COSTS

Most of the cost of high-quality preschool is in the salaries of the teachers and other care-givers. For the Perry Preschool Project, 81 percent of the cost was for teacher salaries. This high cost is also associated with the size of the care groups directly reflected in the teacher/child ratio.

If one teacher and one aide were provided for every fifteen children, the costs (in 1986 dollars) for quality preschool per child would range between $3,500 and $4,000. There are now an estimated 730,000 four-year-olds nationwide who can be considered at risk. Providing them all with quality preschool education would cost between $2.6 and $3.1 billion. [15]

According to the National Day Care Study conducted in the 1970s by Abt Associates, smaller class sizes were associated with desirable classroom behavior and improved cognitive performance. This study was conducted with young children, and it found that the most favorable outcomes were for groups with fewer than sixteen children enrolled, with a maximum group size of twenty, and with an adult-child ratio of one to ten.

In addition, the study found that the only teacher characteristic that predicts program quality and effectiveness was the amount of training in early childhood development and education. However, the current salary and career structure for most child-care workers and preschool teachers is far below that of teachers in K-12 classrooms. The average annual salary of Head Start staff in 1985 was $7,700, substantially below the average $14,500 starting salary for public school teachers and a mere one-third of the average public school salary of $23,546.[16]

YSLETA PRE-KINDER CENTER PROGRAM

As part of the education reform package passed in Texas in 1984, the legislature provided funding for half-day preschool programs for all four-year-olds who were either non-English-speaking or from a low-income family. In the Ysleta District of El Paso, an entire school was set aside for prekindergarten classes that created a "learning laboratory" for teachers and instructional aides. The school accommodated a total of 700 children, with 300 more in a satellite center, and it had an adult-student ratio of 1 to 11.

The Ysleta Program emphasizes five essential areas of development:

- Awareness of language as a means of communication
- The use of the five senses to observe the environment
- Development of motor skills, including physical coordination, balance, and fine motor skills
- Expression of creativity through art, music, and drama
- Social-emotional development by building confidence and self-esteem

The program makes extensive use of field trips; special programs in health, safety, and entertainment; and computers for learning.

An extensive parent-education program provides access to a wide variety of resources and an ongoing support group, and parenting classes are conducted in both English and Spanish. Parents are also encouraged to volunteer in the classroom and in other aspects of the program. Adult literacy is an important part of the Ysleta program, and a library provides books for children to take home to their parents so that the parents can read to them. Also available to parents are free classes in English conversation and citizenship information.

Contact: Ysleta Pre-Kinder Center, 7909 Ranchland Drive, El Paso, TX 79915

Guided by this comparison, we recommend placing a higher value on the skills and services of teachers of preschool and child-care programs than they currently enjoy. The profession should allow for career development similar to that now envisioned for the teaching profession as a whole. It is possible to keep staff expenses down by employing teaching assistants at lower salaries, but these lower-paid personnel should have the opportunity to become fully certified teachers and master teachers within the preschool and child-care fields.[17]

PROGRAM GUIDELINES

Maintaining high standards for preschool programs should be a high priority of policy makers, particularly at the state level, where program guidelines are developed. The following characteristics of quality early education programs have been identified by the High Scope Research Foundation:[18]

- At least one staff member for every ten children and a classroom enrollment limit of no more than twenty children.

- Teaching staff who are early childhood specialists with academic degrees in early childhood development, competency-based child development associate credentials, or their equivalents.

- Curriculum models derived from principles of child development that have been evaluated and found to have positive intellectual and social outcomes.

- Support systems to maintain the curriculum model, including curriculum leadership by administration, curriculum-specific in-service training and evaluation procedures, and teaching staff assignments that permit daily team planning and evaluation of program activities.

- Collaboration between teaching staff and parents as partners in the education and development of children, including frequent communication and substantive conferences at least monthly.

- Sensitivity and responsiveness to the child's health and nutrition requirements and the family's need for child care or other services.

Finally, all preschool programs should provide parenting assistance. According to a report by the National Governors' Association, the "curriculum of the home" is twice as powerful a predictor of academic success as is socioeconomic status.[19] In twenty-nine controlled studies of child-care and preschool programs, the most favorable outcomes were in programs designed to improve the curriculum of the home. The kinds of activities these programs encouraged were conversations between parents and children about everyday events, showing interest in social activities, discussions of reading, monitoring and discussions of television watching, and learning to postpone immediate gratification in favor of long-term goals.

*   *   *

Unless society intervenes early in the lives of children in need, the nation will be forced to confront an expanding pool of young people who are equipped neither to learn nor to work. On both economic and humanitarian grounds, our nation cannot afford to waste valuable human resources by relegating a significant proportion of its children to the underclass.

But in order to be most effective, early intervention programs need to establish a strong link between parent education and child development, stressing the overriding importance of the home curriculum and helping parents to develop higher aspirations for themselves and their children.

Despite the clear positive impact early intervention programs can have on later school achievement, the public schools cannot be expected to carry the entire burden of providing these needed support services. Some activities will be able to utilize existing school structures and trained school personnel. The most obvious of these are schools that work with teenage mothers and their babies. Each community must determine its needs and find ways to link public and private resources and expertise. Funding and program support will need to come from a variety of sources, including federal, state, and local government, corporations, other businesses, and foundations.

Such a broad-scale coalition of public and private resources can do the most to help early intervention and preschool programs reach those disadvantaged children and families who require this support.

CHAPTER THREE

RESTRUCTURING THE SCHOOLS

A primary goal of early intervention is to improve the readiness of disadvantaged children for formal classroom education. But there is little sense in giving disadvantaged children a head start if the schools that await them fail to provide the kind of quality educational programs that can reinforce early successes. Unless the public schools offer skilled and caring teachers and administrators, a safe and inviting environment, a stimulating academic curriculum, and the necessary social supports, society will have wasted its investment in early intervention and cheated its children in the process.

Few schools in disadvantaged communities currently provide a productive educational environment. Dropout rates, the most convenient gauge of school efficacy, typically range from 30 to 50 percent in predominantly poor, minority school districts. In some inner-city schools, dropout rates exceed 80 percent. Of those students who receive high school diplomas, perhaps half have reading and writing skills that are inadequate for the job market.

We believe that schools serving disadvantaged students need to undergo fundamental restructuring if they are to ensure these children access to high-quality education. This will require schools and their communities to reach beyond the traditional boundaries of education in order to provide the comprehensive services and sustained effort needed by disadvantaged children and youths.

Tinkering with school programs will succeed only in patching up some of the cracks of an outmoded education system. Although a few more children may be caught before they are lost to the system, we will fail to bring the majority up to the higher standards now being demanded by society. Incremental reform within the traditional structures of the nation's public schools simply cannot address the critical needs of this substantial segment of our school population.

Of course, not all schools will require the kinds of fundamental change we advocate. Many schools in both affluent and middle-class areas are already performing the educational tasks expected of them and are doing well. However, it is a sad fact that too many schools in disadvantaged communities are failing to provide the majority of their students with the skills they will need to lead successful lives. **Therefore, the restructuring of schools must be made a priority in communities whose children suffer serious problems of poverty and discrimination. Such restructuring will require fundamental changes in the way schools are organized, staffed, managed, and financed.**

SCHOOLS AS FACTORIES

In urban and minority communities, the public schools often serve as a vehicle of alienation rather than education for their disadvantaged students. The school system that was developed at the turn of the century to meet the needs of a newly industrialized nation was modeled after the factories in which students could expect to be employed as adults.

Most schools still follow this factory-style design, even though it no longer provides an effective way to develop the kind of problem-solving skills the nation will need in order to stay competitive. The large size of most urban schools, a compartmentalized approach to learning, and the low expectations of students by staff and administration often make it impossible to provide the sense of belonging and continuity that children from disadvantaged homes — indeed, all children — need in order to prosper.

EDUCATION REFORM AND THE DISADVANTAGED

As discussed in Chapter One, the first wave of education reform generally focused on the educational needs of the majority by advocating higher standards and more of the same — more courses, more homework, a longer school day and year. However, many of these proposals created a new dilemma. Higher standards for all without special support for the disadvantaged would inevitably result in higher failure and dropout rates among those who traditionally labor under the greatest handicaps.

Nevertheless, the issue of dropouts and potential dropouts has not been ignored completely. Much effort has been expended on trying to find ways to keep at-risk high school students in school, and alternative programs have been developed that attempt to reach out to those who have already dropped out of the school system.

Despite these efforts, however, there has been little or no improvement in the dropout rate in the past few years, and for severely disadvantaged children, the situation seems to be getting worse, not better.

We believe that it is necessary to reevaluate existing dropout prevention programs in order to determine which are truly working and which are less than successful, perhaps even harmful. The recent community-wide effort to reexamine the effectiveness of the Boston Compact provides an excellent example of how communities can respond to changing needs. Business leaders, community leaders, and educators from the school system and Boston's higher education network are working together to redirect the Compact's goals toward reducing the city's high dropout rate. (Chapter 4 presents a more detailed description of this effort.)

THE NEED FOR QUALITY TEACHERS

Improving the quality of the teaching profession has become a focal point of a second wave of reform proposals. Although more and better teachers are essential for improving the overall quality of public education, the education system will be facing a severe teacher shortage in the next few years as fewer qualified candidates choose the profession and experienced teachers approach retirement age.[1]

With fewer well-qualified teachers entering the system, it will probably be harder to attract new teachers with good qualifications to inner-city and other disadvantaged areas and keep more experienced teachers from transferring to other schools. School districts caught in a hiring crunch will tend to assign neophyte or underqualified teachers to problem schools, even though the need for better teachers with special qualifications for such schools is apparent. Attracting qualified minorities, who are desperately needed to serve as role models for disadvantaged students, will also become increasingly difficult as higher entry standards disqualify some candidates and other professional opportunities lure away those who are more academically gifted.

THE COMMUNITY SCHOOL

The way schools are organized and run reflects the value society places on the welfare of its children. Excellent schools exist in communities where parents and educators share a belief in the power of education to give their children a good start in life. Where the community devalues education and where parents are ill informed, intimidated by the bureaucracy, or uncaring, there ceases to be a strong constituency for quality public schools. Educators may try their best, but ultimately the children suffer from this lack of community commitment.

It is time to reconsider the role the school must play in the lives of children and the communities in which they live. One way to revitalize the link between school and community is to make schools the focal point for a variety of community activities and social services targeted to children.

As an institution, the public schools provide an ideal physical setting in which to offer a variety of services needed by the large numbers of children who are at risk. They can provide a locus for parenting education, health care, and social activities that involve parents, teachers, children, and other members of the community.

We urge a reevaluation of schools that serve large numbers of disadvantaged children and the assignment of accountability measures to administrators, staff members, and school districts. A new relationship must be developed between the school district and the community that encourages schools to reach out to parents, community members, and business. Public schools and communities must work together to design and tailor programs that meet the special academic, vocational, social, and health needs of disadvantaged children and adolescents.

Early and sustained intervention and support are needed to root out the inequities caused by disadvantage. The positive effects of early compensatory or remedial education often dissipate after one or two years. Providing short-term help without making changes in the negative environment in which most disadvantaged children live usually has no sustained impact on their lives.

We believe that support and continued monitoring of the educational and social progress of disadvantaged youngsters must be sustained from kindergarten through high school if programs are to have the maximum effect. At the same time, state and local governments and school boards must provide the support necessary to enable local schools to meet their educational goals through programs designed to address the specific needs of their students.

THE CURRICULUM OF THE HOME

Many disadvantaged children do not receive reinforcement in their home lives for the positive traits that will lead to future employability. This negative home curriculum is estimated to contribute to about half of the problems students exhibit in school.[2] And even where parents try their best to overcome the negative influences outside the home, their efforts are often defeated by the chaotic conditions prevailing in the community.

Good programs require the active participation of parents. Among other goals, they should teach parents how to provide a home environment that encourages learning. Where the home cannot provide such simple necessities as a quiet place to study, proper nutrition, and warmth and cleanliness, other avenues need to be explored.

Wherever possible, elementary, middle, and high schools should reach out to parents of disadvantaged children and involve them in school activities. The process developed by child psychiatrist James P. Comer in several New Haven, Connecticut, schools involves parents directly in school decision making (see "Redesigning the Inner-City School: The Comer Process," page 44). Not only have there been dramatic improvements in the attendance, behavior, and achievement of the children in those schools, but the parents have developed greater self-confidence and have helped increase the involvement of other parents in school activities.

The involvement of concerned and caring parents also helps to improve communication between parents and children and between parents and teachers, and it creates a sense of belonging often missing in the inner city. It can also be an important deterrent to drug use, delinquency, and teen pregnancy.

EMPLOYABILITY SKILLS AND THE INVISIBLE CURRICULUM

As business leaders, it is not our task to pass judgment on different instructional strategies or on course content. Nevertheless, common sense suggests that among the most important skills students need to develop are those that will enable them to become self-supporting adults, informed citizens, and good parents.

An extensive survey conducted for *Investing in Our Children* identified the skills and attributes that both employers and institutions of higher education consider necessary for success in the workplace and in college.[3] Among those most important for job success were good English-language communication skills, positive work habits, problem-solving ability, and the ability to continue to learn. Not surprisingly, college officials identified the same traits as important to success in higher education.

These skills are transmitted by both the regular school curriculum and its "invisible" curriculum, which consists of the messages the school sends students about what is or is not valued in the adult world in terms of behavior and achievement. *An effective invisible curriculum stresses good work habits, teamwork, perseverance, honesty, self-reliance, and consideration for others. These character-builders are as important to future success as the academic skills taught through the traditional curriculum.*

The invisible curriculum is where the foundations for employability are laid. Schools that develop and reinforce good habits, shared values, and high standards of behavior are most likely to produce graduates who succeed in higher education and work. The foundation for later success should be laid long before kindergarten and should be reinforced throughout the educational process.

BOTTOM-UP MANAGEMENT

Essential to the restructuring of schools is providing individual schools with greater autonomy over the hiring of staff and the development of curriculum and greater responsibility for the educational performance of their students. A number of communities are now experimenting with school-based management programs that reflect the philosophy underlying the bottom-up strategy for school improvement developed in *Investing in Our Children*.

This strategy calls for reform efforts to be focused at the point of learning: the school, the classroom, and the interaction between teacher and student. Among the communities that are instituting such management designs are Miami (see "Miami–Dade County School-Based Management Project," page 46) and Seattle.

Another approach to school-based management that is particularly geared to the needs of disadvantaged children is the one developed by Dr. Comer in the New Haven schools (see below). A significant feature of this model is that it was designed to change the attitudes of school staff toward disadvantaged children and bring parents directly into the school decision-making process. Dr. Comer views the school as the one institution in the inner city that can provide the important stable social network that children need if they are to thrive. The children are not the direct focus of this school-improvement process, but by fundamentally changing the way principals, teachers, other staff members, and parents interrelate, it has helped to improve substantially the academic achievement, attendance, and behavior of the students.

REDESIGNING THE INNER-CITY SCHOOL: THE COMER PROCESS

Dr. James Comer, a psychiatrist at the Yale University Child Study Center in New Haven, has developed an innovative management process that has dramatically improved the educational and social climate in two New Haven elementary schools. Both schools serve a student population that is close to 100 percent black, almost all of whom are economically disadvantaged. As much as 70 percent of the student body comes from homes that receive some form of public assistance.

The pilot project was begun in the Martin Luther King Elementary School in 1968; the Kathleen Brennan School joined the project in 1974. Both schools were ranked at the bottom of New Haven's thirty-three elementary schools and suffered from most of the problems endemic to inner-city schools. The new management process has achieved significant long-term results. The King School is now fifth among all New Haven schools in academic achievement and first in attendance, and the Brennan School has similarly improved.

The Comer Process is a school-based management approach that focuses on changing the attitudes and working relationships of principals, teachers, counselors, health-care professionals, and, most significantly, parents. A management and governance team and a mental health team meet regularly to deal with general and specific school issues and student problems. Although the principal retains his authority, decisions are usually reached by consensus, with the understanding that if the approach chosen does not work, one of the alternatives proposed will be tried.

Team members are rotated yearly to avoid the formation of an elite. The process helps to foster a sense of school ownership among administration,

MAKING SCHOOLS MORE RESPONSIVE

Among the characteristics of schools that contribute to their effectiveness, researchers agree that size is one of the most important.[4] Low-achieving students commonly complain of feeling anonymous within the structure of the typical urban comprehensive high school, which may have as many as 3,500 students. Indeed, even those who perform well in school report negative feelings about their school setting.[5]

A school size of 300 to 400 students and a low adult-to-student ratio have been identified as optimal at the middle and high school levels. Schools of this size are associated with fewer disruptions, higher achievement, higher rates of participation in extracurricular activities, and greater feelings of satisfaction with school life.[6] School size is usually taken into

faculty, and parents. An example of an innovative solution that arose from one school's management team was the decision to have teachers remain with each class for two years. This system has provided continuity in the learning process for children who often have chaotic home lives.

Dr. Comer sees active parent participation as the key to the process. One of the chief functions of the management and governance team is to design and carry out a social activities calendar for the entire school year, with parents playing a primary role. Parents are also encouraged to volunteer in the school as teacher aides. In one case, a parent served as a librarian.

Parents who do not have the time to volunteer during the school day are kept informed of activities through parent-run newsletters, involvement in a strengthened parent-teacher organization, and evening social activities. Parental involvement has grown impressively, and parent turnout for school functions often surpasses expectations. In some cases, the parents have themselves been motivated to return to school and obtain their high school or college degrees.

The long-term nature of the results are worth noting. Schools with severe problems cannot be turned around overnight. This process is now being instituted systemwide in New Haven's schools and in several other school districts around the country, including Prince Georges County, Maryland, and Benton Harbor, Michigan.

Contact: James P. Comer, Maurice Falk Professor of Child Psychiatry, Yale Child Study Center, Yale University, 230 Frontage Street, New Haven, CT 06510 account in the design of alternative schools, many of which have been created in the past decade to respond to the special and diverse needs of at-risk youths in urban areas.

When schools are smaller, there is a greater chance that they can maintain a safe and inviting atmosphere. Smaller schools may also provide an organizational flexibility that will enable them to meet the needs of the individual student. Even for school buildings built to accommodate 1,000 to

---

MIAMI–DADE COUNTY SCHOOL-BASED MANAGEMENT PROJECT

The Miami–Dade County Unified School District recently implemented a unique program in school-based management and shared decision making. Twenty elementary, middle, and secondary schools and nine magnet schools will participate voluntarily in the project, which will run for four years.

Called SBM/SDM for short, this project will provide personnel in each school with the opportunity to implement a learning-centered curriculum designed to meet student needs using a variety of flexible problem-solving strategies.

While enlarging the role of teachers in the decision-making process and providing leadership training to principals and teachers, the project will also involve parents and community members in an advisory capacity.

The first year of the project will be used to select principals and faculties for the pilot schools and develop and utilize a training program for administrative and instructional personnel. The final three years will be used to implement the school-based management model and develop an evaluation process.

One of the unique features of Miami–Dade's program is its development through an unusually close collaboration between the school district and the local teachers' union.

The decision-making process will include budget decentralization, curriculum planning, program planning, collegial decision making, and comprehensive planning as a vehicle for improving school-centered programs and establishing priorities. SBM/SDM is focusing the full resources of the school system at the school level and encouraging decisions at this level so that the best education possible can be realized for all students.

Contact: Joseph A. Fernandez, Superintendent of Schools, Dade County Schools, 1450 N.E. Second Avenue, Miami, FL 33132

5,000 students, alternatives to the current comprehensive high school model are possible. For example, schools might experiment with alternative school models to create a variety of small schools-within-a-school, which could be organized around core programs in different subject areas or could offer students and teachers a nontraditional approach to the normal academic program. Boston is experimenting with such an approach, with large schools being subdivided into smaller units in certain teaching areas.

The benefits are greater awareness of student achievement, more opportunity for teachers to confer with colleagues on particular students' needs, greater coordination of the curriculum so that students receive the appropriate level of instruction in basic and higher-level skills, clearer and fairer disciplinary guidelines, better collegial and peer spirit, and a greater sense of belonging for both teachers and students.[7]

Core programs that focus on subjects such as communications, biological sciences, and finance could draw on businesses in their community to provide a link between academics and the development of practical skills. Business can also help introduce new technologies to the schools and assist in developing appropriate applications and providing materials, creative services, and technical assistance. Computer programs modeled on everyday applications of skills such as word processing can provide a creative approach to learning basic skills. One highly regarded program is IBM's "Writing to Read," which is being used in many elementary school classrooms to teach the creative process of writing while increasing reading skills.

However, few experts believe that technology alone can solve all the problems that beset today's schools. At its best, technology provides an excellent vehicle for teaching and reinforcing a variety of basic and higher-level skills with the learner setting the pace. However, in order for computer-assisted instruction to be really effective, teachers themselves need to be involved with the development of both programs and classroom applications.

A BASIC DESIGN FOR SCHOOLS

No two good schools are necessarily alike. We believe that the American school system benefits from a healthy diversity of school design and offerings. However, despite some significant exceptions, schools that serve the disadvantaged do not work well, especially where they perpetuate the factory model. Accordingly, educators and policy makers need to reassess the elements that make for a successful learning environment for disadvantaged students, whether they are in elementary, middle, or secondary schools. We have found a number of characteristics to be the most important for schools in general and for those serving disadvantaged students in particular.

- **School should be a place where children want to learn.** First and foremost, schools should provide a safe and inviting place for children and adolescents to spend their time. A school that is physically inviting, whose staff believes they are working to a common purpose, and that excludes the negative influences of the outside environment is bound to provide an experience conducive to successful learning.

- **English-language proficiency should be a paramount objective of the school program.** Good communication skills in standard American English are absolutely essential for later employability, and these skills are most readily learned in the early years of childhood. Foreign language studies are important to overall intellectual development, but bilingual programs should have as their goal full English proficiency.

- **Character building through a positive invisible curriculum should be emphasized.** Schools should be conscious of the standards of behavior and achievement they set. Developing positive work habits, interpersonal relationships, and character traits should be a primary goal of all classroom work and extracurricular activities.

- **Teachers should be given a more important role while being held more accountable for student progress.** Teachers of disadvantaged students have a special mission in the classroom beyond the teaching of subject matter. They provide role models and continuity for children who often do not have adults to emulate in their home environment.

All teachers should receive appropriate training in child and/or adolescent development in addition to the rigorous academic training we are now coming to expect. This is particularly vital for elementary and middle-school teachers, who often confront children with a wide range of emotional and physical problems.

Teachers should be brought more fully into the decision-making process of the school. More attention should be paid to the concepts of team teaching and mentoring, particularly at the elementary and middle-school levels, as a way of helping to relieve the isolation experienced by teachers and to provide a more integrated approach to learning.

Teachers should be held accountable for results and rewarded for performance through an appropriate set of evaluation procedures and incentives. At the same time, districts should provide ongoing educational opportunities for teachers that specifically address the teaching of disadvantaged students. Such education and training could most effectively be provided either by the district itself or in collaboration with local schools of education.

In Chapter 4 of *Investing in Our Children*, CED recommended "nothing less than a revolution in the role of the teacher and the management of the schools." Recommendations that we believe can enhance the professional role and increase the responsibilities of teachers are contained in that report.[8]

■ **Principals need to develop better leadership and management skills.** Most good schools have good principals at the helm. Unfortunately, many principals lack the necessary leadership and management skills. Most have received little support from their school systems in terms of management education and training. The task of the principal is to provide a positive environment within which teachers are free to teach to the best of their abilities. Principals need to provide open lines of communication both within the school and with parents, business people, and others in the community.

Business can make a valuable contribution by providing training for principals in the fundamentals of management. Some companies, such as IBM, and school districts such as Miami–Dade County and Washington, D.C. (see "The D.C. Management Institute," page 50) are currently providing such training to principals. **We recommend that the business community create more such management academies to help educators hone the skills they will need to manage schools more effectively.**

■ **Schools should encourage greater parental involvement.** This is the key to improving the educational prospects of disadvantaged children. Particularly at the elementary and middle-school levels, parents should be brought into the school decision-making process. They should be encouraged to work in the classroom as aides and to interact more frequently with their children's teachers.

Parents need support from employers to be able to participate more fully in their children's education. Not all children in need live in welfare-dependent homes. Many have one or two parents who work as hourly employees at low-wage jobs. These parents have little flexibility to attend school functions or teacher conferences that must be held during the day. Employer support through release time or flexi-

---

THE D.C. MANAGEMENT INSTITUTE

In 1983, Floretta Dukes McKenzie, superintendent of the Washington, D.C., public schools, initiated contact with local businesses to solicit their help in training school administrators to improve managerial planning and decision making in noneducational, noncurricular activities. By 1984, the D.C. Management Institute was created with eleven corporations participating on the advisory board. The program operates through Dr. McKenzie's executive assistant for corporate affairs, Dr. Robert Carleson, and has been designed in three stages:

- Stage 1 — Twenty-four participants were selected for the first management program. The needs of participants — principals and school managers with systemwide responsibilities — provided the guiding force in designing the program. Instructors with particular areas of expertise were drawn from the private sector.

- Stage 2 — This stage is currently under way. Those who have completed the initial program are brought back to learn how to teach the curriculum to others. It is anticipated that eventually corporate trainers will be eliminated from the program. In addition, the second stage involves a practical application of the knowledge gained in the program via a project designed by the participants in their own administrative area.

- Stage 3 — This stage is still under development. It is planned that school administrators and corporate chief executive officers and other private-sector managers will gather to work on a series of case studies that focus on a variety of educational problems.

Initial reports from participants indicate that the program is achieving its goals. Specifically, the D.C. Management Institute has helped principals and other administrators to manage their personnel more effectively, has made participants more aware of the problems in other areas of the district, has helped establish a community orientation among participants, and has narrowed the perceived gap between the public and private sectors through cooperation.

Contact: Floretta D. McKenzie, Superintendent, Washington, D.C. Public Schools, 415 12th Street, N.W., Washington, D.C. 20004

SOURCE: *American Business and the Public School: Case Studies of Corporate Involvement in Public Education,* eds. Marsha Levine and Roberta Trachtman (New York: Teachers College Press). Forthcoming.

ble working hours would greatly increase the ability of at-risk children to profit from more active parental involvement.

■ **Extracurricular activities should become a more important part of school programs.** Many disadvantaged children have single parents who work or two parents who work full time. Some have no parental guidance whatsoever or are responsible for the care of younger children. And those who do have adequate adult supervision can nonetheless benefit from enrichment activities outside of the normal classroom setting.

Extracurricular activities build school spirit and provide a place for latchkey children to spend profitably the hours between the end of the school day and their parents' working day. They also provide important invisible curriculum lessons and a variety of new physical, intellectual, and cultural challenges for which there may not be time during the academic day. We believe that these activities can provide a critical counterpoint to the boredom and idleness that often lead to drug use and other negative behavior.

Such activities can provide both supervised learning and study opportunities, formal educational offerings that go beyond the regular curriculum, or sports, drama, and other worthwhile recreational pursuits. Many of these activities can be jointly sponsored by the schools, community groups, and even businesses.

■ **Comprehensive health and social services are needed to address problems that interfere with learning.** Disadvantaged students seldom have the family resources to respond to such needs as preventive health care, nutritional guidance, and psychological and family counseling. The efficiency and effectiveness with which these services could be delivered would be much greater if they were centralized at the school building level.

Although disadvantaged children have a higher incidence of health problems and malnutrition, many receive their only contact with medical services in the emergency room of a local city hospital. The school nurses who run many in-school health services are becoming indispensable members of the educational team at many inner-city schools. They often have more personal contact with students and understand students' needs better than many teachers or parents do.

The need for school-based health care is underscored by the rising pregnancy rate for girls between the ages of eleven and fourteen and the growing use of drugs, alcohol, and other controlled substances among children in this age group. In-school health services are an appropriate mechanism through which to provide sex education, pregnancy prevention programs and follow-up services, and substance abuse programs. In the area of birth control information and services, each school should work with parents and others in the community to design a health services program that conforms to specific community needs, values, and standards.

Sometimes these comprehensive services are best provided at an alternative site within the community. One such model with a long record of success is the Door, located in New York City and supported by a variety of private and corporate foundations (see "The Door: Services for Adolescents," page 53).

COMPENSATORY EDUCATION IN THE ELEMENTARY SCHOOLS

The elements of good school design apply equally to elementary, middle, and high schools. In addition to these kinds of structural elements, we believe a word on behalf of remedial education programs at the elementary level is needed. Chapter I reading and mathematics programs have over the past twenty years helped to narrow the achievement gap between disadvantaged and nondisadvantaged students. However, because of inadequate funding, only 40 to 50 percent of children eligible for this program have participated in it. **We endorse the continuation of Chapter I remedial programs and recommend that the federal government bring their funding up to levels sufficient to reach all eligible children.**

MIDDLE SCHOOL: MAKING THE TRANSITION

Middle and junior high schools represent a major transition for young adolescents between the ages of eleven and fifteen. This is a time of great change and exploration, when youngsters are becoming more receptive to learning abstract concepts and higher-order intellectual skills.

Middle school represents a critical point in the education of disadvantaged children. For many, the gains that were made in elementary school are dissipated during the middle-school years for reasons that are still unclear. This is the point at which dropping out is apt to occur, particularly for children who have had to repeat grades.

Middle schools remain the neglected alleyway of education reform. They are truly schools in the middle, with identities that are unclear to the

THE DOOR: SERVICES FOR ADOLESCENTS

The Door is the largest comprehensive health, educational, and cultural service center in the nation. Designed to serve New York City's disadvantaged youth, it was founded in 1972 under the auspices of the International Center for Integrative Studies. The Door is an alternative center that provides a range of free social services for youths from age twelve to twenty. Activities are designed to address physical, emotional, intellectual, and interpersonal problems. Services include:

- **Educational and Prevocational Preparation** — Remedial education, career counseling, and prevocational training.

- **Creative and Physical Arts** — Visual, performing, and plastic arts programs; martial arts and competitive sports.

- **Health Center** — Primary medical care; health promotion, sexual health and awareness, prenatal care and education; nutrition and food services.

- **Mental Health and Social Services** — Prevention; intervention/treatment; substance abuse treatment.

- **Social and Legal Services** — Crisis intervention; emergency support; representation in legal proceedings.

Activities take place in a large renovated department store that has been designed as a counterpoint to traditional educational and service facilities, which the directors feel have alienated many inner-city youths. Teens may hear about The Door from friends or may be referred by teachers, principals, or the courts. They are free to participate in any of its programs regardless of the reason for their initial visit.

The Door's whole-child approach to adolescent development has attracted attention locally, nationally, and internationally. It receives requests for training in providing comprehensive services from human service professionals, administrators, and other youth professionals. It has served as a model for similar centers in New York City, New York State, Washington, D.C., Mexico, Guatemala, Canada, the Virgin Islands, Australia, and the Philippines.

Contact: The Door — A Center for Alternatives, International Center for Integrative Studies, 618 Avenue of the Americas, New York, NY 10011 students who attend them, the faculties and administrators who staff them, and the public that funds them. Nothing illustrates this lack of identity better than the various terms that are used for these schools, including *middle schools, junior high schools,* and *intermediate schools.* There is no consensus on what grades should be encompassed. Depending on the community in which they are located, middle schools may serve grades five through eight, six through eight, or seven through nine. In some cities, such as New York, different middle schools follow different grade structures.

The traditional concept of the middle school was to provide a special setting for the educational transition of early adolescence. The separate school was designed to act as a bridge between the single-teacher, single-class environment of elementary school and the multidiscipline, multi-teacher setting of the typical comprehensive high school.

Over the years, the blurring of organizational lines between junior high and high school eroded the intended purpose of middle schools, which was to provide a unique educational approach to the developmental needs of early adolescence. For teachers, too, middle school became a way station to high school certification and assignment, rather than a sought-after credential in its own right. Prospective elementary school teachers generally receive training in child development. But middle schools are usually considered secondary education, and no special credential or training in early adolescent behavior is required.

THE NEGLECTED ALLEYWAY

Despite the intensity of the nation's education reform movement, middle and junior high schools have been largely ignored. Most reform studies, beginning in 1983 with *A Nation at Risk,* focused on increasing standards and course requirements at the high school level. A few reports, such as the U.S. Department of Education's *First Lessons,* have examined the need for reform at the elementary level.

In *Investing in Our Children,* CED assigned junior high and middle schools a high priority for reform. **In light of the slow progress on behalf of schools in the middle, we believe even more strongly that junior high and middle schools — and the children who attend them — should be a major focus of education reform. We also urge that these schools become the subject of new and comprehensive research and scrutiny. If not, it is doubtful that successful reform can be implemented.**

There have been several recent promising developments. The John Hancock Insurance Company last year created an endowment of $1 million for use in twenty-two middle schools in Boston, with the funds earmarked for a broad range of innovative academic and intramural athletic programs.

In addition, a new center on middle schools has recently been established at Johns Hopkins University, and the Center for Early Adolescence at the University of North Carolina–Chapel Hill is involved in extensive work on effective middle-school programs. The Lilly Endowment is spearheading a Middle Grades Improvement Program in selected school districts in Indiana. The goal of this program is to bring school and community resources together to plan in a collaborative process and possibly implement school and after-school programs that provide a coherent learning environment for middle-school students.

FUNDAMENTALS OF GOOD MIDDLE SCHOOLS

In New York City, the New York Alliance for the Public Schools recently completed a study of fourteen junior high schools that have clearly improved the educational achievement of their largely minority student bodies. The study pointed to five important characteristics that these successful junior high schools had in common:[9]

1. Strong leadership from the principal, which included a sense of mission and the ability to allocate resources.

2. Solid structure and curriculum, including an emphasis on extracurricular activities.

3. A positive image that helped attract students and staff.

4. The development of a strong teaching and support staff.

5. A system of accountability, rewards, and incentives for both students and staff.

More research in diverse communities could more precisely identify the unique needs of at-risk junior high school students. However, preliminary discussion with those who work in junior high schools indicates that students would benefit most if their schools undertook some of the same structural changes that we believe all public schools need, albeit tailored for the particular developmental needs of the young adolescent. We suggest the following points of emphasis for middle and junior high schools:

■ **Smaller schools, smaller classes, and more individualized instruction.** In elementary school, students spend each year with one teacher and the same classmates. One of the most jarring aspects of the transition to middle school is getting used to departmental programs, five or six different teachers, and many more classmates.

It is in junior high that many students, particularly in large urban schools, begin to feel a great sense of anonymity, isolation, and alienation. Some successful junior high schools in the New York study solved this problem by dividing the student body into different schools-within-a-school, where students in each group shared the same group of teachers for all their subjects. This also provided an opportunity for the teachers to plan better and coordinate their lessons with those of their colleagues teaching different subject matter.

■ **Better guidance counseling.** Few large urban schools have adequate guidance staffs. As a consequence, their time is usually confined to crisis intervention and such activities as special education placement. Disadvantaged middle-school students need much more in-school guidance than their more affluent peers, but they seldom have adequate counseling. It is increasingly important that low-income, minority youths receive guidance on higher education and future careers in middle school so that they and their parents can make more informed decisions about the preparation they will need in high school. Long-range employment counseling is an area in which businesses can make a contribution through volunteer career counselors and mentors.

■ **Greater parental involvement.** Direct parental participation in school activities tends to decline after elementary school. This phenomenon can be clearly seen in the smaller numbers of parents who belong to parent-teacher organizations in junior high and high schools. Yet early adolescence is a critical time to maintain parental connections to the school, especially for parents of children who are at risk of becoming dropouts or otherwise failing.

■ **Specialized teacher training and recruitment.** Middle schools need to be regarded as a special place in which teachers can have a rewarding career. They need to shed their image as a way station for teachers seeking high school credentials or appointment. Middle-school teachers should have specialized training in early adolescent development, and there should be separate middle-school credentials. In addition, these schools need to recruit teachers who have a special affinity for working with the whole child and with young adolescents.

The business community has an important stake in improving the quality of middle and junior high schools. This is where we lose a substantial proportion of the disadvantaged population. The basic skills not learned by middle school are more difficult and more expensive to inculcate during high school or on the job. The business community can play an important role in partnerships with the schools by providing adult role models, mentors, and tutors, as well as participating in the guidance process through release time for employees.

HIGH SCHOOL: KEEPING AT-RISK STUDENTS IN THE CLASSROOM

Low-achieving students tend to get lost in the enormity of the average urban high school. Special programs, more individualized instruction, and work experience related to their academic tasks will encourage these students to remain in school and learn valuable skills. Where vocational education is an important part of the curriculum, it is valuable only where it is of high quality, modern job skills are taught, and academic instruction is an integral part of the program.

In addition to the principles of school structure already discussed, we believe the following would be of particular value to at-risk students in the high schools:

■ **Alternative schools within the larger high school structure.** Successful models for alternative schools have been pioneered in a number of troubled communities. An excellent example is Middle College High School in New York City (see "Middle College High School," page 58). Alternative schools and programs that are organized around a particular core academic or vocational area have also shown considerable success in keeping dropout-prone youths interested in pursuing their education. These programs tend to create a new sense of identification for students and teachers, increase teacher and student accountability, and reduce the sense of alienation most low achievers experience.

■ **Improved guidance counseling.** In addition to the need for more qualified guidance counselors, we see three specific areas where the guidance function for at-risk students needs to be improved:

— Employment and career opportunities

— Post-secondary school placement

— Psychological needs and family problems

Business can provide additional guidance, especially in the area of employment and career opportunities and the preparation needed for more advanced careers.

■ **Mentoring programs.** Students who are dropout-prone or chronic low achievers generally come from backgrounds that provide very limited interaction with successful adults. Mentoring programs, such as those run by the New York Alliance for the Public Schools in advertising and law, expose disadvantaged students to important new experiences and provide contacts within the world of work. There are now many impressive examples of successful mentoring programs around the country. A notable example is Ogilvy and Mather's graphic arts program (see page 79).

■ **Meaningful work experiences.** Low-achieving students need greater exposure to the world of work, both as an incentive to stay in school and as a way of broadening their life experiences. However, it is critical that such work be more than a supplement to income. Research has shown that many forms of adolescent work experience can be detrimental to school performance and only serve to reinforce the sometimes negative values of peers.

Work experiences provided by internships, cooperative education programs, or vocational education programs should relate directly to what is being taught in school and should help to reinforce basic academic and

---

MIDDLE COLLEGE HIGH SCHOOL

Founded in 1974, Middle College High School is a New York City alternative public high school that is affiliated with La Guardia Community College, located in Long Island City. To qualify for admission, a student must have a high rate of truancy, multiple academic failures, or come from a troubled home. Yet for each entering tenth-grade class, there are now 600 applicants. Admission selections are made collectively by the principal, guidance counselors, and a committee of graduating seniors.

With 500 students, the school is small; the average class has 20 students. The small scale allows teachers and administrators to follow up on students. For instance, if a student has difficulty getting up in the morning, the school will arrange a wake-up call. The principal, Celia Cullen, has noted that "very few kids disappear here."

Four full-time counselors lead eleven daily group sessions with about a dozen students in each group. Although students receive no credit for these sessions, they appreciate the opportunity to communicate with peers and caring adults to discuss issues such as drugs, sex, and family problems.

When students enter Middle College High, they receive a La Guardia College identification card. However, the connection to the college is not the main point. More important is the sense of responsibility that is developed through self-pacing and flexible schedules that permit students to accommodate personal and family needs.

Because of its impressive results with hard-to-educate youths (the graduation rate is about 85 percent), Middle College is serving as the model for three new alternative schools in New York City as well as six sites around the country.

Contact: Celia Cullen, Principal, Middle College High School, Long Island City, NY 11101

SOURCE: *The New York Times,* "Dramatic Drop in Dropouts," December 5, 1986.

higher-level problem-solving skills. Educators should work with business leaders in their community to create work experience opportunities, design vocational and cooperative education programs, and provide feedback and guidance in their ongoing operation.

Business can also provide summer jobs for disadvantaged youths to help them earn needed money, provide valuable work experience that does not impinge on academic classwork, and in some cases, provide academic learning opportunities along with the work assignments. Summer Training and Education Program (STEP), a national demonstration project run by Public-Private Ventures in five cities around the nation, is using a combination of summer jobs, life skills, and basic skills education to help improve the chances that at-risk students will complete their education (see "Summer Training and Education Program," page 60).

■ **Extracurricular activities.** Sports, drama, school government, and a variety of nonacademic activities serve an important function for all children, especially those at risk. After-school jobs, which are increasingly common among middle-class teenagers, are much scarcer for minority youth, even though they have a greater need for the extra money. Too much free time disposes teens to boredom and experimentation with drugs, sex, and crime. Schools can and should provide alternatives after regular school hours. Many extracurricular activities are student-directed and offer lessons in leadership and initiative, as well as teamwork and creativity. The advisory role of teachers in many of these activities also presents adults in roles that are different from those they play during the day, providing a basis for new, more flexible relationships between teachers and students.

REENTRY FOR SCHOOL DROPOUTS

The final link in the chain of programs to meet the needs of the disadvantaged are those that address the problems of potential dropouts and encourage those who have already dropped out to improve their basic academic and job skills and obtain their high school degrees.

This group of students is generally the most difficult to reach effectively. Retention rates for participants in employment programs have not been encouraging, especially over the long term. One of the problems often identified by experts working with severely disadvantaged dropouts is the short-term nature of many of the programs. Funding usually lasts for a limited demonstration period, and resources are not generally available for continued tracking of participants.

The most successful programs for retrieving dropouts are those that link work experience with instruction in basic skills. The best track record for

60

long-term gains by participants belongs to the Job Corps, a residential program providing a mixture of skills training, remedial education, improved motivation, and health care. The residential setting allows intensive attention to participants' problems and progress away from the distracting setting of their neighborhood environment.

Because of the comprehensive nature of the program, Job Corps is expensive, costing more than $15,000 a year per client. However, if policy

---

SUMMER TRAINING AND EDUCATION PROGRAM

The Summer Training and Education Program (STEP) is a national demonstration project initiated with Ford Foundation support and managed by Public/ Private Ventures, a Philadelphia-based research and program development organization. The program is designed to increase high school graduation rates among disadvantaged youth by addressing two root causes of dropping out: poor academic performance and adolescent parenthood. STEP provides low-income youths who are potential dropouts with a combination of remedial reading and math instruction, life skills, school-year support activities, and work experience in conjunction with Summer Youth Employment and Training Programs in five cities: Boston, Fresno, Portland (Oregon), San Diego, and Seattle.

Now in its third year, STEP will reach some 2,250 youths over a four-summer period. Target youths are fourteen- and fifteen-year-olds who are doing poorly in school and are economically eligible for the federally funded Summer Youth Employment Program in their communities. The program will include long-term follow-up of participants and comparison with a control group (who participate in summer jobs but without the remedial education) to determine the impact the program has had on high school graduation rates, childbearing, and early labor market experience.

Research shows that STEP youths of both sexes and all racial groups, in all five demonstration sites, scored higher in math and reading, were more likely to be promoted during the school year, were more informed about sexually responsible behavior, and were more likely to use contraception than were control group youths. Over the summer, non-STEP youths had lost about a full grade in reading and one-half grade in math, while STEP youths lost only slightly more than one-third of a grade in reading and gained one-third of a grade in math. STEP youths increased their knowledge of the consequences of teen parenting and how to avoid pregnancy; those who were sexually active were one and a half times more likely to have used contraception than sexually active non-STEP youths.

Contact: Public/Private Ventures, 399 Market Street, Philadelphia, PA 19106

makers consider the alternatives, which often include incarceration at an estimated $30,000 a year, the cost-effectiveness of Job Corps and similar programs becomes apparent. From the perspective of taxpayers, programs of this type are a sound investment in view of the long-term benefits of reduced criminal activities, decreased welfare payments, and higher contributions to the tax system from participants.

Another approach to improving basic skills among both dropout-prone youths and those who have already left school is being tried by the Remediation and Training Institute through its computer-based Comprehensive Competencies Program (CCP). This program, which utilizes the latest technologies, offers a complete training package for the local agencies, schools, and organizations that provide the actual delivery of services.

Jobs alone, however, do not provide the necessary motivation for dropouts to change their lives. Most long-term results of supported work programs have been disappointing. The Manpower Demonstration and Research Corporation (MDRC), which pioneered this concept, reassessed the structure of such programs and developed a variation in which remedial education and skills training are added to the highly structured work experience that characterizes supported work. Although funding was withdrawn after only one year of operation, the redesigned program had encouraging early results, especially in the retention of participants and the percentage who go on to unsubsidized jobs or future education or training.[10]

Evaluations of the California Conservation Corps (CCC), which is a community service program, are beginning to indicate that programs based on this model can have some positive impacts on the employment rates and income levels of at-risk participants. Unfortunately, the relative newness of this and similar programs has made it difficult to ascertain their long-range impact on young people who are most at risk. An early study of attrition rates for the California program found that those who did best in the short run were youths who already have higher levels of education. Dropout-prone youths had high attrition rates and either left voluntarily or were dismissed before the end of the twelve-month program.

However, further studies of CCC now in progress seem to indicate that all program participants, both those identified as at risk and those from more stable backgrounds, are showing gains in income and employment relative to a control group one full year after participation in the program. The follow-up study also seems to indicate that at-risk youths who participated in the CCC have developed more positive attitudes about themselves and their communities as a result of their experiences.[11] Further analyses of the CCC and other community service programs that recruit at-risk youths bear watching.

Another organization that has had some success with at-risk youth is the Youth Action Program, located in East Harlem, which provides both comprehensive educational services and training in skills needed in the job market.

For those who have already dropped out of school and who do not have adequate basic skills, the future is grim. Programs that attempt to work with the most estranged youths without addressing their multiple skill and life deficiencies have shown very limited success. However, some lessons can be extracted from the experience of these programs that are important to keep in mind as existing programs are redesigned or new ones are created.

■ Programs need to combine education in basic skills and work in a setting that relates the two.

■ Programs are best offered in an alternative setting that removes participants from their troubled environment so that they can concentrate on improving motivation and skills.

■ Youngsters who desire to return to the education system to complete high school are best served by alternative schools that are small and provide targeted services in a setting that helps to build self-esteem.

Most of all, programs designed to address the needs of disadvantaged youth need continuity and long-term funding. Critical to long-term success is the provision of follow-up services that keep in touch with participants after they leave the program and evaluate their progress. So far, this is the major missing element in dropout retrieval programs.

*   *   *

All children must have access to quality basic education, but this ideal is often very difficult to achieve in high-poverty areas. One reason is that the constituency for school reform tends to be weaker in these communities than in middle-class areas because parents of disadvantaged children usually feel powerless to effect change.

Meeting the needs of the whole child must become a hallmark of public education. This will require a restructuring effort that effectively changes the way we think about our schools and their function within the community. Schools need to be smaller and less compartmentalized. They should offer a broad array of social and health services to both children and their families. They should be staffed with responsive, caring, and highly qualified teachers and administrators.

Restructuring the schools will mean taking teachers out of their isolation and providing them with greater opportunities to make decisions, share responsibility, and interact with other teachers and education professionals. It will mean greater parental involvement in the schools and in their children's education. It will mean engaging business in a more active relationship with the schools and the community.

The school years must become part of a learning continuum that begins at birth and continues throughout life. We must reach beyond the traditional boundaries of public schools to provide an early and sustained involvement with children and their families. In this way, the schools will gain a new vitality, and society will be certain that no needy child is overlooked.

CHAPTER FOUR

SCHOOLS, BUSINESS, AND THE COMMUNITY: PARTNERSHIPS FOR CHANGE

In recent years, corporations have demonstrated a growing commitment to improving the public school system. School-business partnerships, ranging from adopt-a-school programs to public advocacy, have multiplied across the nation.[1] But business and the schools face a larger challenge: to demonstrate the same commitment to resolving the increasingly serious problems of the educationally disadvantaged.

The guidelines for successful corporate involvement in the problems of high-risk students are similar to those designed to improve public schools generally. First, successful partnerships must have specific mutual goals. Each partner should fully understand what the other has to offer, and each should have a realistic view of what might be accomplished. Second, partnerships should engage students, teachers, school administrators, parents, business executives, and others in the community in a collaborative effort that is focused on improving the performance and self-esteem of students, developing their talents, and strengthening their relationships with peers and adults.

BEYOND TRADITIONAL BOUNDARIES

As this policy statement illustrates, the problems of children in need call for collaborations that must extend beyond the traditional limits of the schools. For example, solid preparation for education and employment must begin in the earliest years of life, long before formal schooling takes place. Older students at risk will require a wide range of social services both in the school and the community.

As a strong community force, business can help bring together a wide variety of interested parties — schools, parents, community groups, and government agencies — to explore opportunities for creating new partnerships or strengthening those that already exist. Corporations can also help guide the use of public and private resources in directions that represent sound investment strategies. Most of all, business leaders can become a persuasive voice for the millions of disadvantaged children who lack advocates in the political process. Business leaders must speak out on behalf of the educationally disadvantaged because these children cannot speak out for themselves.

Currently, most school-business partnerships take the form of adopt-a-school programs. Such linkages serve the important purpose of bringing a business and an individual school closer together, and they should be encouraged. Individual schools and their students derive important benefits from their corporate partners, and the participating business executives often speak of the knowledge and satisfaction they gain from their personal involvement with students, teachers, and parents.

Despite these obvious advantages, past experience indicates that adopt-a-school programs have had a limited effect on the performance of students at risk. Most adopt-a-school programs have been focused at the high school level, although a greater need exists in both the middle and elementary schools for closer ties with business and the experiences it can offer. Furthermore, adopt-a-school programs can sometimes become an easy substitute for a more sustained and far-reaching corporate commitment to public education for disadvantaged children.

Effective school-business partnerships for the educationally disadvantaged call for leadership from the highest ranks of business and education. At their best, such partnerships establish a process as well as a program. They foster substantive long-term relationships and cooperative efforts that involve school personnel, corporate employees, parents, community leaders, and elected school officials in an effort to define problems, establish goals, and develop sound strategies for investment.

Successful partnership efforts are already under way in the three major categories that we believe represent effective investment strategies for improving the performance of the educationally disadvantaged: *prevention through early intervention, restructuring of basic schooling,* and *targeted programs for retention and reentry.*

PREVENTION THROUGH EARLY INTERVENTION

Research studies indicate a clear need to place greater emphasis on preventing problems among at-risk children from prenatal care to age five. Such preventive approaches require the active participation of both the children and their parents because the parents are often young, poor, and in need of help themselves. One promising new program for providing intensive and comprehensive support to at-risk mothers and their children from prenatal care to age five is the Beethoven Project in Chicago (see "The Beethoven Project," page 67). The program's premise is that if children are to achieve success in later years, they must be ready for school when they enter kindergarten.

The Minneapolis Business Community Employment Alliance, an organization of business, government, and civic leaders chaired by Mayor Donald M. Fraser, was formed in 1983 to address the problem of long-term unemployment. As the Alliance studied the difficulties of hiring the hard-to-employ, it realized that obstacles to employment stem mainly from a lack of job skills, poor health, and other handicaps and that for most hard-to-employ adults, these problems begin long before adulthood.

The root of the problem, the Alliance found, was in the early years of social and intellectual development, which strongly influence academic performance and work skills. The Alliance appointed a Future Employability/Early Childhood Development Task Force. Its report, *Preventing Unemployment: A Case for Early Childhood Education,* urges business, government, and civic leaders in Minneapolis and throughout the country to start to work with disadvantaged children at birth to ensure their employ-ability as adults. Minneapolis is now in the planning stages for a "Five Plus" program for children from prenatal care to age five.

THE BEETHOVEN PROJECT

One of the most innovative projects designed to help children in need is taking place in Chicago. The Beethoven Project provides prenatal care to expectant mothers so that their children will have a better start and a better chance for success when they enter Beethoven Elementary School. The project also teaches young mothers basic parenting skills and emphasizes their own and their children's need for basic education.

Funding for this project comes from a combination of government and pri-vate sources. Irving B. Harris, a Chicago business leader, has pledged $600,000 for the next three years, matching a grant from the Federal Depart-ment of Health and Human Services, and state and city agencies will make substantial contributions to the project. Developmental programs for infants and toddlers will be available to all children born in the Beethoven Elementary School enrollment area. Head Start programs will also be made available to all children when they reach three years of age. In addition, fulfilling health care and nutritional needs for the children will have a high priority.

The project, operated by the Ounce of Prevention Fund and sponsored by the Chicago Urban League, is unusual because it will provide comprehen-sive care for a large group of children over a five-year period. Thus far, it has demonstrated success in its ability to mobilize human resources; it works within a circumscribed community using community people for whom intensive training is provided. Trained home visitors inform expectant moth-ers of available health care, family counseling, and other services.

The Beethoven Project generates a high degree of personal commitment from the project's directors and operational staff, the local high school prin-cipal, and a community advisory council. It will take time to ascertain whether this program will dramatically improve teaching and learning in the Beethoven School. It is also expected to improve health, reduce delin-quency, and curb the growing problem of teenage pregnancies in inner-city poverty areas. It is an impressive innovation that merits national attention and perhaps widespread replication. Governor James R. Thompson of Illi-nois has already announced plans to develop several similar projects in other localities.

Contact: The Ounce of Prevention Fund, 188 W. Randolph, Suite 2200, Chicago, IL 60601

CHILD CARE

A study financed by AT&T demonstrates that worker satisfaction and productivity are related to employees' ability to provide competent child-care arrangements. Accordingly, many corporations are beginning to recognize the need to make a variety of quality child-care services available to their employees.

The knowledge that their children are in a safe, healthy, and educational environment can help parents concentrate more fully on their work without having to worry that they are jeopardizing the development of their children. This is particularly important for potentially at-risk and single-parent families. Recently there has been an increase in the number of companies supporting resource and referral services for their employees. For example, IBM began offering a free child-care referral service to 240,000 employees in 1984, and 14,000 families have used it so far.[2]

In addition, corporations have been financing recruitment of new child-care workers, arranging employee discounts at local day-care centers, paying child-care providers directly, or adding money to employees' paychecks to pay for child care. The California Child Care Initiative, started by the BankAmerica Foundation, has recruited, trained, and helped certify 230 people who provide care for over 1,000 children across the state. Funding for the program has come from fourteen corporations and the public sector. Despite a growing commitment to assisting employees with child-care needs, corporations can provide only part of the needed funds. As the California example indicates, the public sector must commit resources for child-care facilities as well, particularly for preschool-age children from at-risk families.[3]

RESTRUCTURING BASIC EDUCATION

One way business can assist the educationally disadvantaged is to support projects that improve basic education through programs that reach beyond education's traditional confines. Company-sponsored projects can give students valuable insights into the world of work while teaching the basic skills of reading, writing, and arithmetic. They can also provide a valuable mentoring experience to disadvantaged and minority students who can benefit greatly from the interaction with successful adult role models.

In order to promote higher-quality public school education in Atlanta, the business community joined forces with public school officials to form the Atlanta Partnership of Business & Education (see page 69). This organization sponsors several programs that enable the business community to

ATLANTA PARTNERSHIP OF BUSINESS & EDUCATION

A broad-ranging school-business partnership is the citywide Atlanta Partnership of Business & Education, Inc. Organized in 1981, this nonprofit corporation is designed to further the educational opportunities of the city's 68,000 students and to assist the Atlanta Public School System.

During the 1985–1986 school year, the Partnership focused its resources on the following five programs:

- **Adopt-a-School,** which is operated by the Partnership and pairs individual schools and businesses.

- **Affirmative Action/Adopt-a-Student,** which was developed and is operated by the Merit Employment Association, an organization of about forty Atlanta businesses. The program pairs business volunteers with individual junior and senior high school students who are at risk of not graduating.

- **Distinguished Scholars–Humanities,** which with the National Faculty Humanities Program helps link university faculty and teachers from the Atlanta schools.

- **Institutionalization,** which represents an effort by a business task force to raise funds to endow a chair at Georgia State University that will promote school-business partnerships.

- **Volunteers/Tutorial,** which links volunteer tutors from religious institutions and businesses with schools that seek tutorial services.

In addition to supporting these programs, the Partnership provides internships for students, helps plan school curricula, and gives managerial assistance to the schools.

The organization's commitment to public education extends beyond the Atlanta community. In 1984, the Partnership successfully lobbied for the passage of Georgia's Quality Basic Education Act, comprehensive education reform legislation designed to improve the public school system throughout the state.

Contact: Boyd Odom, Executive Director, Atlanta Partnership of Business & Education, Inc., University Plaza, Urban Life Suite 736–739, Atlanta, GA 30303

SOURCE: Bernard J. McMullen, et al., *Allies in Education: Schools and Businesses Working Together for At-Risk Youth* (Philadelphia: Public/Private Ventures); and Atlanta Partnership of Business & Education, Inc., Atlanta, GA.

target at-risk youths. Common to all these programs is a fundamental emphasis on upgrading basic education.

Corporate involvement in improving basic education does not need to be launched on a large scale to be effective. For example, a small amount of money distributed to inner-city schools can greatly improve the way basic education is delivered. These discretionary funds to individual schools or to teachers in the form of minigrants can be used to support innovative proposals that would not be feasible without some increases in funding. Corporate funding of special projects can grant schools a degree of autonomy in developing and implementing methods to improve the basic education of all students.

LOCAL EDUCATION FUNDS

An important phenomenon has been the recent expansion of local education funds. A local fund acts as an intermediary developing community support for and private-sector involvement in public school systems. These funds have also mobilized community leadership and raised private dollars for minigrants to teachers and other programs to improve local school systems.

The success of local education funds sparked the formation of the non-profit Public Education Fund (PEF) in 1982, which has awarded grants to forty-three local funds so far in an effort to establish or strengthen public-private collaboration on behalf of public schools with high enrollments of disadvantaged youngsters. During PEF's five-year life, local funds supported by it have made major strides toward self-sufficiency by receiving matching funds from community sources at a ratio of almost five local dollars for every dollar provided by PEF.

One broad-scale effort along these lines that involves local business, the community, and the public schools is *Forward in the Fifth* in rural Kentucky's Fifth Congressional District, one of the poorest and most disadvantaged in the nation. An umbrella organization for the entire district, *Forward in the Fifth* is working to establish affiliates in each of the district's counties through technical and financial support (see page 71).

TARGETED PROGRAMS FOR RETENTION AND REENTRY

Until recently, school-business partnerships have had little impact on the dropout problem. But organized activity spurred by business leadership is now under way in major cities across the country. Boston represents a model of business and community collaboration on behalf of dropout prevention and reentry. The Boston Compact is an agreement among business, education, and community leaders to improve educational performance and reduce the dropout rate in exchange for jobs in the private sector. It has organized a communitywide response to Boston's worsening dropout problem (see page 72).

The Boston Compact is being used as a model in other cities and states for business-school partnerships that are designed to link improvements in academic achievement with job opportunities. Massachusetts has undertaken the expansion of the Compact model in five other cities, and both New York and New Jersey are using the design in statewide efforts. In addition, Baltimore and Cleveland have established or are in the process of

---

FORWARD IN THE FIFTH: A COMMUNITY PARTNERSHIP FOR RURAL KENTUCKY

Kentucky's Fifth Congressional District, located in the southeastern part of the state, is one of the poorest sections of the nation, and its public schools consistently rank among the lowest in achievement. In a concerted effort to combat problems of low achievement and high dropout rates, a group of business, education, and community leaders met in the fall of 1986 to launch a districtwide organization called *Forward in the Fifth*.

Forward in the Fifth hopes to establish a local affiliate in each of the school district's twenty-seven counties by the end of 1988. The umbrella organization will provide both technical and financial assistance to each affiliate to help it accomplish a number of important goals: enriched education for pupils; increased involvement by parents and businesses; greater innovation by teachers and principals; recognition of outstanding achievement by students, teachers, and principals; greater communication between schools and the community; and increased confidence in and commitment to the schools.

Forward in the Fifth has organized several advisory councils of key groups, including higher education, school superintendents, school board members, and teachers. The organization also has a newsletter to keep members and affiliates informed and to highlight local programs, events, and awards. To encourage the development of local affiliates, *Forward in the Fifth* launched a yearly matching grant campaign through which it will match contributions raised by the local groups up to a total of $1,500. In this way, each affiliate could obtain as much as $3,000 per year to establish a minigrant program, business partnerships, and attendance improvement or other school improvement programs.

Contact: "Forward in the Fifth," 210 Center Street, Berea, KY 40403

developing programs that replicate key aspects of the Compact, and a new project funded by the U.S. Department of Health and Human Services and the National Alliance of Business (NAB) will attempt to recreate the Com-

---

THE BOSTON COMPACT:
A COMMUNITY RESPONSE TO THE DROPOUT PROBLEM

In September 1982, the Boston Public Schools and leaders from local government, business, labor, higher education, and the community began a collaborative effort through the Boston Compact to improve the education available to Boston's young people. Since implementation of the Compact, public school attendance has improved significantly, as have reading and math scores, and a competency-based graduation requirement in reading has been established.

Boston's school-to-work transition effort, jointly run by the school system and the Boston Private Industry Council, filled 2,600 summer jobs in 1986; its goal for 1987 is 2,800 jobs. In 1985, the program placed over 900 graduates in full-time jobs in the private sector. Colleges and universities have created a network of support organizations to increase college attendance, and area building trade unions are committed to an annual 5 percent increase in the number of graduates entering union apprenticeship programs. However, the goal of reducing the dropout rate has not been met. In the 1985-1986 school year, over 3,000 high school students dropped out. Between their freshman year and graduation, 43 percent of the class of 1985 left school.

A recent conference sponsored by the Boston Compact, the Boston Private Industry Council, State Street Bank and Trust Company, the Federal Reserve Bank of Boston, and the Committee for Economic Development provided a forum for the sustained discussion of a dropout-prevention and reentry plan presented by Schools Superintendent Laval S. Wilson. In order to correct the current problems, the plan suggested changes in the way schools are organized, program innovations in basic education, alternative programs, social and human services in the community, and a funding strategy that involves a public-private, state-local collaboration. The plan was subsequently adopted and financed; a supplementary $2 million commitment in August 1986 was funded equally by the mayor's office and the Boston School Department. The program puts special emphasis on teacher involvement, student support teams, alternative education, and parent outreach. The Boston Compact itself has broadened its scope in order to bring it into closer touch with middle schools and community organizations.

Contact: Edward Dooley, Executive Director, The Boston Compact, 26 Court Street, Boston, MA 02108.

pact's essential elements in seven cities — Albuquerque, Cincinnati, Indianapolis, Louisville, Memphis, San Diego, and Seattle — while adapting it to meet local conditions and needs. The Boston Compact Steering Committee and the NAB will provide technical assistance to these cities.

In the absence of sufficient individual support and caring, many at-risk students eventually leave school before graduation. When traditional support is unavailable, business can work with local schools to develop innovative programs that show concern for each at-risk student.

One such program is Rich's Academy, an alternative high school in Atlanta for dropouts or low-achievers who have difficulty functioning in the normal school setting. It is located in Rich's Department Store, a major local business institution. To develop the Academy, Rich's worked with both the local public schools and Cities in Schools (see page 74), a national organization that helps provide comprehensive support services to schools. Rich's donates the space for the schools and encourages employees to volunteer. Currently, 160 employees of Rich's and other Atlanta businesses volunteer to help with after-school programs, tutoring, and social services. In addition to regular academic work, the Academy offers work-study opportunities and social services through Exodus, Inc., the local organization that manages the Cities in Schools program. Rich's has also adopted four other schools in Atlanta and sponsors an Adopt-a-Friend program that links adult volunteers with individual students.

Another program that is designed to provide personal attention to at-risk students is the Valued Youth Partnership (see page 75), sponsored by Coca-Cola in San Antonio, Texas, which uses cross-age tutoring to deter students from dropping out and builds new, caring relationships with · schools, communities, and families.

PERSONAL RELATIONSHIPS

Some of the most successful school-business partnerships have reached young people directly through personal relationships. Individual commitment, personal involvement, and the incentive of direct financial support are hallmarks of the "I Have a Dream" Program, initiated by Eugene Lang, founder of the Refac Technology Development Corporation, in New York City. These have been major factors contributing to redirecting the lives of a group of at-risk inner-city students in East Harlem.

In 1981, while delivering a graduation speech to a class of sixty-one sixth graders at P.S. 121, Mr. Lang decided to abandon his planned exhortation to work hard and succeed and instead offered each child who graduated from high school a scholarship to cover the cost of college tuition. Fifty of the original students are expected to graduate from high school, and approximately one-half will pursue higher education.

Mr. Lang recognized that the promise of a scholarship alone would not be enough, and therefore hired a project director to follow the progress of the students and to work with them individually. He also spends more than just money; he devotes his personal time to provide a "family" support system to these children.

CITIES IN SCHOOLS: SUPPORT SYSTEMS FOR STUDENTS AT RISK

Founded in 1975, Cities in Schools is the largest national nonprofit organization devoted to dropout prevention. This public-private partnership headquartered in Washington, D.C., is supported by a variety of private businesses, foundations, and individuals with matching funds from a federal interagency grant. It has more than 60 local dropout prevention programs in 23 cities serving at-risk students and their families.

Cities in Schools believes that a student's decision to drop out of school can stem from one of many factors, including family tensions, drug and alcohol abuse, delinquency, illiteracy, and teenage pregnancy. It identifies problems underlying the dropout phenomenon such as abuse, neglect, undernourishment, and emotional stress that occur outside of school but affect in-school performance. Cities in Schools views students holistically and addresses their interrelated problems in a coordinated and integrated fashion, assembling in one place a support system of caring adults who ensure that students have access to the resources that will help them rebuild their self-esteem and academic skills to prepare them for productive futures.

The Cities in Schools process brings existing social services into schools where they can most benefit at-risk youth. To achieve this at the local level, Cities in Schools brings together local government, school officials, and business representatives in partnership to form a board of directors. This local board assesses its community's needs, and then hires a privately funded facilitation team, trained to act as a broker in the needed services to an education site. The goal is to establish a prototype at such a site that can then be replicated communitywide. During the local development process, the national office of Cities in Schools provides training and technical assistance.

Cities in Schools has been forging and continues to forge public and private partnerships with organizations such as Boys Clubs of America, VISTA, United Way, and Junior League, as well as the Departments of Justice, Labor, Health and Human Services, and Education.

Contact: Bill Milliken, President, Cities in Schools, Inc., 1023 15th Street, N.W., Washington, D.C. 20005

Mr. Lang's initial offer has spawned a high degree of interest both from school systems and from other individual philanthropists. Out of this groundswell of enthusiasm grew the "I Have a Dream" Foundation, whose purpose is to help others replicate the program and provide the necessary motivation and support to give meaning to the pursuit of a college education. So far, Mr. Lang's initiative has provided the model for similar scholarship programs funded by businesses or individuals in New York, Boston, Cleveland, Chicago, Dallas, and other major cities. In Dallas, enough money has been pledged to guarantee college tuition for at least 1,000 disadvantaged youngsters. The program is now in place in fifteen cities, involving 100 different sponsors and 4,000 students. The "I Have a Dream" Foundation expects this number to double by the end of the year.[4]

Nevertheless, Mr. Lang himself is cautious about the long-term effects of his program. He knows that a scholarship alone does not provide sufficient incentive for at-risk youths to make it through school. Accordingly, he

---

COCA-COLA VALUED YOUTH PARTNERSHIPS: PROGRAMS IN CARING

The Valued Youth Partnership (VYP) program in San Antonio, Texas, cosponsored by Coca-Cola and the Intercultural Development Research Association, is designed to help middle and high school students who are potential dropouts. The basic goals of the program are to keep students in school and improve their academic achievement.

The program identifies high-risk students as valued youth and gives them an opportunity to serve as tutors of younger children. Peer tutoring is a teaching-learning process with learning, friendship, and social growth as its outcomes. As the student-tutors care for and teach younger children, they learn as well.

Two years after implementation, the VYP program has achieved extraordinary success: absenteeism declined; only six percent of the students in the program dropped out of school compared to 37 percent in the county; tutors' grades, self-image, and behavior improved; and parents demonstrated enthusiasm and support for the program. Crucial to the success of the program have been role modeling, parental involvement, curriculum development, and student recruitment. The success of the VYP program demonstrates the importance of building school, family, and community relationships to prevent high-risk students from leaving school.

Contact: Jose A. Cardenas, Director, Intercultural Development Research Association, 5835 Callaghan, Suite 350/111, San Antonio, TX 78228

calls for a comprehensive support system to provide the motivation to succeed. Furthermore, he believes that private aid to the schools cannot substitute for public financing.

MENTORING PROGRAMS

Disadvantaged youths often lack appropriate adult role models and sufficient contact with caring adults who can offer the encouragement they need to succeed in school. In cities where it plays a major role in the life of the community, the U.S. Navy participates in many partnership programs that feature mentoring activities and one-to-one relationships between navy personnel and schoolchildren. In many cases, these activities benefit the naval personnel as much as the children with whom they interact (see "The U.S. Navy and America's Schools: A Shared Commitment," page 77).

EDUCATION AND EMPLOYABILITY: MEETING MUTUAL NEEDS

The issue of employability has proven to be a powerful bond between schools and businesses and a means by which small businesses, in particular, can join in partnership with the schools. Jobs give young people a sense of purpose and an important connection with the outside world. Young people from disadvantaged homes often lack knowledge about the world of work, have few positive adult role models, and have limited access to the job market. Businesses can provide valuable real-world experience for these youths and offer the role models they lack. In addition, appropriate job experience can help teach or reinforce the basic skills in which disadvantaged youth are so often deficient. **Businesses need to intensify their involvement with the schools through summer jobs programs, cooperative education, mentoring programs, vocational education, and job placement programs.**

Some of the most effective job-related partnerships combine mentoring with job training in specific marketable skills. One such example is the graphic arts program developed by Ogilvy and Mather, one of the nation's largest advertising agencies (see page 79).

CORPORATE POLICIES, CORPORATE FUNDING

Leadership from the top is essential if a corporation is to make a serious long-term commitment to helping to solve the problems of the educationally disadvantaged. Moreover, policies established by the corporation in response to these problems need to permeate the entire organization. We

THE U.S. NAVY AND AMERICA'S SCHOOLS:
A SHARED COMMITMENT

In many American cities, the U.S. Navy is one of the largest employers and a major economic force. Recognizing its commitment to the community at large and the important role naval personnel can play as resources and role models, the navy has embarked on successful and innovative partnerships in education at the elementary, junior high, and secondary levels. Currently, the navy sponsors three programs.

■ **Adopt-a-School** — When the 231 officers and enlisted men of the tank landing ship USS *Bristol County* decided to adopt a San Diego junior high school, they formed a partnership in education that soon reached other ships and shore-based commands. Through these focused programs, sailors share their skills in a wide variety of areas both in and out of the classroom. From academics to sports, school projects to community activities, these navy men and women have found ways to become contributing members of a community far from their homes.

■ **The Math/Science Initiative** — Officers, senior enlisted personnel with technical training, and retirees volunteer their time and knowledge to provide computer instruction to teachers and students, judge science fairs, serve as club sponsors, and tutor individual students. Personnel nearing retirement can also pursue a specially designed program leading to full certification and a second career in teaching. The program was begun in Pensacola, Florida, and has expanded to Orlando, Jacksonville, and Mayport, Florida; Corpus Christi, Texas; Great Lakes, Illinois; Norfolk, Virginia; Memphis, Tennessee; San Diego, California; and Bremerton and Bangor, Washington.

■ **Saturday Scholars** — This program, which began in 1983 as a partnership between the Chicago Public School System and the Naval Training Center at Great Lakes, Illinois, is now active in many cities across the nation. Elementary school students who want to improve their reading and mathematics skills report to their schools on six consecutive Saturdays. Carefully screened sailors tutor the children on a one-to-one basis. Although emphasis is on strengthening basic skills, the students also benefit from the individual attention of caring adults. Widely praised wherever it is in place, the Saturday Scholars program reflects the navy's growing commitment to the education of our nation's youth.

Contact: Director, Pride, Professionalism, and Personal Excellence, Naval Military Personnel Command, Washington, D.C. 20370-5000 recommend three areas for special attention.

First, corporate policies can help attack the problems of the educationally disadvantaged by promoting employee participation in local school district activities. **We urge corporations to inform employees of local educational issues and provide opportunities for sustained involvement.**

Although business has traditionally been represented on local and state school boards, business participation at these levels has dropped sharply in recent years. As drawbacks to serving, business executives often cite the long hours, harassment from interest groups, bureaucratic and regulatory interference, and the inability to measure results. [5] We are convinced, however, that the will to serve the community as an advocate for the interests of children can override these factors, especially in the case of younger business executives with children in the public schools. Corporations need to identify such executives and provide incentives for them to serve.

The business community needs to participate in the local and state policy-making process. **Corporate policy should encourage participation on school boards by qualified corporate leaders and key managers.**

Second, corporations can encourage the involvement of parents, a key factor in student success, in their children's education. **We recommend that corporations provide release time and flexible schedules for employees who must attend to their children's educational needs or who want to serve their local school system as volunteers. Such corporate support is especially important for hourly and other nonmanagerial employees who are limited in their ability to arrange time to attend teacher conferences or participate in school functions without being penalized on the job.**

Third, business leaders have an important opportunity to lend their expertise and that of their managers to the design and implementation of programs to assist at-risk students. **We recommend that corporate policies encourage executives experienced in management, research and development, and human resources to apply their talents to the problems of the educationally disadvantaged.**

ADVOCACY FOR THE PUBLIC SCHOOLS

The prestige and influence of the corporate community can be persuasive in arguing the case for increases in public financing of quality schools where needed, special programs to assist the disadvantaged, and fundamental reform of public education. We believe this is an appropriate way for the business community to lend its support to the school system and broaden the concept of traditional partnerships.

Particularly at the state level, local business leaders have been instrumental in spurring systemwide reform and initiating specific programs tar-

OGILVY AND MATHER: MENTORING IN THE GRAPHIC ARTS

In 1976, Ogilvy and Mather, a top national advertising firm, began a partnership with Roberto Clemente High School, in Chicago's inner city, to train students for entry-level positions in their graphics department. The program was conceived both as an opportunity for Ogilvy and Mather to find a good source of young graphic artists and as a way for a small number of talented students in Clemente's two-year art, photography, and printing program to gain experience in the graphics business.

The program began with the selection of eight students, who were paid $3.50 an hour to work five afternoons a week for fifteen weeks. They were taught skills that would make them employable in the graphic arts industry upon graduation. Later, all eight were hired for full-time jobs at Ogilvy. The success of the first class led the teachers from Clemente and the executives from Ogilvy and Mather to institutionalize the program. Students who graduate from the program and then are employed full time by the firm act as mentors for new apprentices. Graduates also teach a marketing class at the high school.

The success of the partnership led to the creation of the Communications Industry Advisory Council, which involves related corporations in the Chicago area with local schools. The council members, currently numbering fifteen, provide a variety of resources, including part-time jobs for training high school seniors, state-of-the-art equipment, and guest lecturers.

The program has been extended to the Ogilvy and Mather office in New York, which has formed a partnership with James Monroe High School, located in a low-income area of the Bronx. Like Clemente, Monroe already had an outstanding art program. The firm is therefore able to draw from a pool of talented individuals, students are taught a marketable skill, and the school has increased its visibility to other potential corporate partners.

The program costs little in terms of direct financial outlays, but strong bonds of commitment have been formed between the company and the school. Some Monroe graduates have been hired as full-time employees at Ogilvy and Mather's New York office; and when a fire destroyed the school's library, Ogilvy employees donated more than 2,500 volumes to replace those lost.

Contact: Marsha Cooper, Senior Vice President and Director of Personnel, Ogilvy and Mather Adv., 676 North St. Clair, Chicago, IL 60611

SOURCE: Roberta Trachtman, consultant to CED.

geted to the disadvantaged. The efforts of the California Roundtable in the early 1980s to assess the quality of public education, help design reform legislation, and ensure its passage and funding in the state legislature are well known. In other states and cities, business leaders have followed California's example. In Washington State, the Washington Roundtable worked with the governor to assure passage of legislation to fund preschool for disadvantaged children. In West Virginia, the statewide business roundtable took part in a historic meeting to guide the future of public education in the state. Similar efforts have taken place in Arkansas, Florida, South Carolina, Texas, Minnesota, and other states.

Individual business leaders are now speaking out at the local, state, and national levels for increased attention to the needs of the disadvantaged. In the federal arena, business leaders have testified before Congress on behalf of increased funding for Chapter I remedial reading and mathematics programs in the elementary schools. **We applaud their efforts and urge other corporate leaders to follow their example.**

The development and implementation of the investment strategies we recommend in this policy statement will require significant increases in funding. Although individual businesses have found opportunities for direct support of the school system, we believe business cannot and should not be viewed as a significant source of funding for public education beyond its important role as a responsible taxpayer in the community.

There are, however, many ways in which business can become directly involved in the funding of schools and programs for the educationally disadvantaged. For example, corporate funds can be leveraged with private foundation funds to broaden opportunities to assist children in need. Moreover, corporations should continue to play a major role in establishing and supporting intermediaries, such as local education funds, that provide innovative programs to assist students at risk. **We urge intensified support of local education funds and other intermediary organizations that are addressing the problems of at-risk students.**

*　　*　　*

In the changing landscape of public education, business has clearly emerged as a key participant. But neither business nor education alone can meet the challenge posed by the millions of children who each year experience failure instead of success in our public schools. What is needed is a broad coalition of business, education, parent organizations, civic groups, and all levels of government working together and generating the political will to accomplish the task. More fully developing the talents of our children in need and simultaneously improving their lives represent the best investment this nation can make in its future.

ENDNOTES

CHAPTER ONE

1. Committee for Economic Development (CED), *Investing In Our Children: Business and the Public Schools* (New York: 1985), pp. 24, 49-50.

2. CED, *Investing in Our Children*, p. 60.

3. Irwin S. Kirsch and Ann Jungeblut, *Literacy: Profiles of America's Young Adults* (Princeton: National Assessment of Educational Progress, 1986); and "Study Links Poor Writing Ability to Lack of Higher-Order Skills," *Education Week* 4:14 (December 10, 1986), p. 1.

4. James S. Catterall, *On the Social Costs of Dropping Out of School* (Stanford Education Policy Institute, School of Education, Stanford University, December 1985), p. 17.

5. Nathaniel M. Semple, "The Urgent Business Role in School Reform," *Atlantic Bell Monthly* (August 1986), pp. 1-3.

6. Henry Levin, *The Educationally Disadvantaged: A National Crisis* (Philadelphia: Public/Private Ventures, 1985), p. 8.

7. Andrew Hahn, Jacqueline Danzberger, and Bernard Lefkowitz, *Dropouts in America* (Washington, D.C.: Institute for Educational Leadership, 1987), p. 2.

8. Daniel Patrick Moynihan, *Family and Nation* (San Diego: Harcourt, Brace, Jovanovich, 1986), pp. 52, 95-97.

9. *U.S. Children and Their Families: Current Conditions and Recent Trends,* a report of the Select Committee on Children, Youth, and Families, U.S. House of Representatives (Washington, D.C.: U.S. Government Printing Office, 1987), p. 28.

10. Greg J. Duncan and William L. Rodgers, *The Prevalence of Childhood Poverty*, Survey Research Center, The University of Michigan, mimeo, 1985.

11. Moynihan, *Family and Nation*, p. 93.

12. *U.S. Children and Their Families*, pp. 13 and 28.

13. "Single Parents Head 25% of Families in U.S.," *The New York Times*, November 6, 1986.

14. Jean G. McDonald, "Readiness for the New Educational Standards," *Time for Results: Task Force on Readiness* (Washington, D.C.: National Governors' Association Center for Policy Research and Analysis, August 1986), p. 14.

15. Harold L. Hodgkinson, *All One System* (Washington, D.C.: The Institute for Educational Leadership, 1985), pp. 5-9.

16. Hodgkinson, *All One System*, pp. 5-9.

17. Hodgkinson, *All One System*, p. 7.

18. *Opportunities for Success: Cost-Effective Programs for Children, Update 1988,* a Report of the Select Committee on Children, Youth, and Families, U.S. House of Representatives (Washington, D.C.: U.S. Government Printing Office, April 1988).

19. *A Better Start: New Choices for Early Learning,* ed. Fred Hechinger (New York: Walker and Company, 1986), p. 156.

CHAPTER TWO

1. Irving B. Harris, address to the National Governors' Association Committee on Human Resources Conference on "Focus on the First 60 Months," February 6, 1986.

2. Lawrence J. Schweinhart and Jeffrey J. Koshel, *Policy Options for Preschool Programs*, High/Scope Early Childhood Policy Papers published in collaboration with the National Governors' Association (Washington, D.C.: 1985), pp. 27-29.

3. *Safety Net Programs: Are They Reaching Poor Children?*, a report of the Select Committee on Children, Youth, and Families, U.S. House of Representatives (Washington, D.C.: U.S. Government Printing Office, December 1986).

4. David A. Hamburg, *Reducing the Casualties of Early Life: A Preventive Orientation* (New York: Carnegie Corporation of New York, 1985), p. 6.

5. Jean G. McDonald, "Readiness for the New Educational Standards," *Time for Results: Task Force on Readiness* (Washington, D.C.: National Governors' Association Center for Policy Research and Analysis, August 1986), p. 60.

6. National Center for Clinical Infant Programs, *Who Will Mind the Babies?* (Washington, D.C.: 1984).

7. Interview with Caroline Gaston, principal, New Futures School, Albuquerque, New Mexico; Frank F. Furstenberg, Jr., *Unplanned Parenthood* (New York: Free Press, 1976).

8. Julie Kosterlitz, "Split Over Pregnancy," *National Journal* (June 21, 1986), p. 1539.

9. Caroline Gaston; and Charles Stewart Mott Foundation, *Teenage Pregnancy: An Update and Guide to Mott Foundation Resources*, 1986, pp. 2-3.

10. *Moving Forward: Next Steps*, Second Report on the Governor's Task Force on Adolescent Pregnancy, State of New York, January 1986, p. 23.

11. Stanley Greenspan, Testimony before a Select Committee on Children, Youth, and Families, U.S. House of Representatives, June 30, 1983.

12. Schweinhart and Koshel, *Policy Options for Preschool Programs*, p. 16.

13. Schweinhart and Koshel, *Policy Options for Preschool Programs*, p. 16.

14. Gary Natriello, Aaron Pallas, and Edward McDill, "In Our Lifetime: The Educationally Disadvantaged and the Future of Schooling and Society," unpublished research paper prepared for the CED Subcommittee on the Educationally Disadvantaged, May 1987.

15. Allen Odden, "State Policy for At-Risk Children: Preschool to High School," *Time For Results: Task Force on Readiness* (Washington, D.C.: National Governors' Association Center for Policy Research and Analysis, 1986), p. 52.

16. Schweinhart and Koshel, *Policy Options for Preschool Programs*, p. 19.

17. Schweinhart and Koshel, *Policy Options for Preschool Programs*, pp. 19-20.

18. Schweinhart and Koshel, *Policy Options for Preschool Programs*, pp. 27-29.

19. Odden, "State Policy for At-Risk Children," p. 52.

CHAPTER THREE

1. *A Nation Prepared: Teachers for the 21st Century*, report of the Task Force on Teaching as a Profession, Carnegie Forum on Education and the Economy, (New York: May 1986), pp. 26-32.

2. Odden, "State Policy for At-Risk Children," p. 52.

3. CED, *Investing in Our Children*, pp. 14-19.

4. Edward L. McDill, Gary Natriello, and Aaron M. Pallas, "A Population at Risk: Potential Consequences of Tougher School Standards for Student Dropouts," *American Journal of Education* 94:2 (February 1986), p. 157-159.

5. National Coalition of Advocates for Students, *Barriers to Excellence: Our Children At Risk* (1985), p. 40.

6. McDill, Natriello, and Pallas, *A Population at Risk*, p. 157.

7. Gary G. Wehlage, "At-Risk Students and the Need for High School Reform," unpublished paper prepared for the National Center for Effective Secondary Schools, School of Education, University of Wisconsin-Madison, May 1986.

8. CED, *Investing in Our Children*, pp. 59-80.

9. New York Alliance for the Public Schools, *Programs and Policies that Work: Helping Schools in the Middle*, May 1986, pp. 64-69.

10. Manpower Demonstration Research Corporation, *Findings on Youth Employment* (New York: 1986).

11. *The California Conservation Corps: A Report on Attrition* (Philadelphia: Public/Private Ventures, December 1986).

CHAPTER FOUR

1. See *Investing in Our Children: Business and the Public Schools*; and *American Business and the Public School: Case Studies of Corporate Involvement in Public Education*, eds. Marsha Levine and Roberta Trachtman, (New York: Teachers College Press), forthcoming.

2. "Day Care Finds Corporate Help," *The New York Times*, January 5, 1987.

3. "Day Care Finds Corporate Help."

4. The "I Have a Dream" Foundation, 31 W. 34 Street, New York, NY 10001.

5. *School Boards: Strengthening Grass Roots Leadership* (Washington, D.C.: Institute for Educational Leadership, 1986), pp. 18, 51.

MEMORANDA OF COMMENT, RESERVATION, OR DISSENT

Page 4, DONALD M. STEWART

While there is absolutely no question that additional resources are requisite to solving this problem, we must also ensure that they are well utilized. We have to have a workable plan for greater coordination and cooperation among the dizzying number of current and potential actors: federal, state, and local governments; education, training, welfare, and economic development systems; public and private sectors; and the various levels of schooling.

Page 14, DONALD M. STEWART

In the context, basic skills should include both educational and work skills. Work experience programs are excellent for providing training in the world of work. However, students should also have the opportunity to gain other skills that will give them an advantage on the job market (clerical skills, computer repair, auto mechanics, drafting, etc.). The specifics could be formulated in conjunction with local businesses.

Page 15, ROBERT A. CHARPIE, with which FRANKLIN A. LINDSAY has asked to be associated

For 25 years public education has sought to implement strategies aimed at helping disadvantaged children within the conventional framework of school systems. We have preferred not to identify problem children by setting them organizationally aside from the mainstream of the system in order to give them special care and separate attention.

I do not quarrel with this societal judgment, although I am personally prepared to advocate any social structure for education, however difficult it may be to accept on societal grounds, which, when rigorously tested, succeeds in educating our disadvantaged children.

This report forces on us courses of action which will separate our disadvantaged children from the mainstream group most of the school day. Nowhere in the report is this issue discussed. I cannot judge whether such separation will be acceptable to those who have led the charge for homogenization of everything in public education. But, it is an issue and it warrants careful consideration and discussion lest the good ideas contained herein go untested in a storm of rancorous social debate.

We wish to give special thanks to the following foundations and companies whose generous support made this policy statement possible.

NYNEX Foundation
Carnegie Corporation of New York
Exxon Education Foundation
Lilly Endowment, Inc.
Charles Stewart Mott Foundation
Pittway Corporation Charitable Foundation
The Ford Foundation
The Standard Oil Company
Brand Companies

OBJECTIVES OF THE COMMITTEE FOR ECONOMIC DEVELOPMENT

For over forty years, the Committee for Economic Development has been a respected influence on the formation of business and public policy. CED is devoted to these two objectives:

To develop, through objective research and informed discussion, findings and recommendations for private and public policy that will contribute to preserving and strengthening our free society, achieving steady economic growth at high employment and reasonably stable prices, increasing productivity and living standards, providing greater and more equal opportunity for every citizen, and improving the quality of life for all.

To bring about increasing understanding by present and future leaders in business, government, and education, and among concerned citizens, of the importance of these objectives and the ways in which they can be achieved.

CED's work is supported strictly by private voluntary contributions from business and industry, foundations, and individuals. It is independent, non-profit, nonpartisan, and nonpolitical.

The 225 trustees, who generally are presidents or board chairmen of corporations and presidents of universities, are chosen for their individual capacities rather than as representatives of any particular interests. By working with scholars, they unite business judgment and experience with scholarship in analyzing the issues and developing recommendations to resolve the economic problems that constantly arise in a dynamic and democratic society.

Through this business-academic partnership, CED endeavors to develop policy statements and other research materials that command themselves as guides to public and business policy; that can be used as texts in college economics and political science courses and in management training courses; that will be considered and discussed by newspaper and magazine editors, columnists, and commentators; and that are distributed abroad to promote better understanding of the American economic system.

CED believes that by enabling business leaders to demonstrate constructively their concern for the general welfare, it is helping business to earn and maintain the national and community respect essential to the successful functioning of the free enterprise capitalist system.

RESEARCH ADVISORY BOARD

STATEMENTS ON NATIONAL POLICY
ISSUED BY THE RESEARCH AND POLICY COMMITTEE

SELECTED PUBLICATIONS

Children in Need: Investment Strategies for the
  Educationally Disadvantaged *(1987)*

Toll of the Twin Deficits *(1987)*

Reforming Health Care: A Market Prescription *(1987)*

Work and Change: Labor Market Adjustment Policies in a
  Competitive World *(1987)*

Leadership for Dynamic State Economies *(1986)*

Investing in Our Children: Business and the Public Schools *(1985)*

Fighting Federal Deficits: The Time for Hard Choices *(1985)*

Strategy for U.S. Industrial Competitiveness *(1984)*

Strengthening the Federal Budget Process:
  A Requirement for Effective Fiscal Control *(1983)*

Productivity Policy: Key to the Nation's Economic Future *(1983)*

Energy Prices and Public Policy *(1982)*

Public-Private Partnership: An Opportunity for Urban Communities *(1982)*

Reforming Retirement Policies *(1981)*

Transnational Corporations and Developing Countries: New Policies for a
  Changing World Economy *(1981)*

Fighting Inflation and Rebuilding a Sound Economy *(1980)*

Stimulating Technological Progress *(1980)*

Helping Insure Our Energy Future:
  A Program for Developing Synthetic Fuel Plants Now *(1979)*

Redefining Government's Role in the Market System *(1979)*

Improving Management of the Public Work Force:
  The Challenge to State and Local Government *(1978)*

Jobs for the Hard-to-Employ:
  New Directions for a Public-Private Partnership *(1978)*

An Approach to Federal Urban Policy *(1977)*

Key Elements of a National Energy Strategy *(1977)*

Nuclear Energy and National Security *(1976)*

Fighting Inflation and Promoting Growth *(1976)*

Improving Productivity in State and Local Government *(1976)*

*International Economic Consequences of High-Priced Energy *(1975)*

  Broadcasting and Cable Television: Policies for Diversity and Change *(1975)*

Achieving Energy Independence *(1974)*

A New U.S. Farm Policy for Changing World Food Needs *(1974)*

Congressional Decision Making for National Security *(1974)*

*Toward a New International Economic System:
   A Joint Japanese-American View *(1974)*

More Effective Programs for a Cleaner Environment *(1974)*

The Management and Financing of Colleges *(1973)*

Strengthening the World Monetary System *(1973)*

Financing the Nation's Housing Needs *(1973)*

Building a National Health-Care System *(1973)*

*A New Trade Policy Toward Communist Countries *(1972)*

High Employment Without Inflation:
   A Positive Program for Economic Stabilization *(1972)*

Reducing Crime and Assuring Justice *(1972)*

Military Manpower and National Security *(1972)*

The United States and the European Community:
   Policies for a Changing World Economy *(1971)*

Improving Federal Program Performance *(1971)*

Social Responsibilities of Business Corporations *(1971)*

Education for the Urban Disadvantaged: From Preschool to Employment *(1971)*

Further Weapons Against Inflation *(1970)*

Making Congress More Effective *(1970)*

Training and Jobs for the Urban Poor *(1970)*

Improving the Public Welfare System *(1970)*

Reshaping Government in Metropolitan Areas *(1970)*

Economic Growth in the United States *(1969)*

Assisting Development in Low-Income Countries *(1969)*

*Nontariff Distortions of Trade *(1969)*

Fiscal and Monetary Policies for Steady Economic Growth *(1969)*

Financing a Better Election System *(1968)*

Innovation in Education: New Directions for the American School *(1968)*

---

*Statements issued in association with CED counterpart organizations in foreign countries.

CED COUNTERPART ORGANIZATIONS IN FOREIGN COUNTRIES

Close relations exist between the Committee for Economic Development and independent, nonpolitical research organizations in other countries. Such counterpart groups are composed of business executives and scholars and have objectives similar to those of CED, which they pursue by similarly objective methods. CED cooperates with these organizations on research and study projects of common interest to the various countries concerned. This program has resulted in a number of joint policy statements involving such international matters as energy, East-West trade, assistance to developing countries, and the reduction of nontariff barriers to trade.

CE	Círculo de Empresarios Serrano Jover 5- 2° Madrid 3, Spain
CEDA	Committee for Economic Development of Australia 139 Macquarie Street, Sydney 2001, New South Wales, Australia
CEPES	Europäische Vereinigung für Wirtschaftliche und Soziale Entwicklung Reuterweg 14,6000 Frankfurt/Main, West Germany
IDEP	Institut de l'Entreprise 6, rue Clément-Marot, 75008 Paris, France
経済同友会	Keizai Doyukai (Japan Committee for Economic Development) Japan Industrial Club Bldg. 1 Marunouchi, Chiyoda-ku, Tokyo, Japan
PSI	Policy Studies Institute 100, Park Village East, London NW1 3SR, England
SNS	Studieförbundet Näringsliv och Samhälle Sköldungagatan 2, 11427 Stockholm, Sweden